PENGUIN BOO.

HEAVENS AND EARTH

Garima Garg is a journalist and an author. Born and brought up in Delhi, she studied economics at Delhi University and attended Columbia University for her MS in Journalism. She writes about culture and her work has been published in various Indian and international publications over the years. In her spare time, she can be found travelling or experimenting as a photographer with her digital, film, and polaroid cameras. She lives with her family in Delhi.

HEAVENS AND EARTH

The Story of Astrology
Through Ages and Cultures

◆ ✶ ◆ ✶ ◆ ✶ ◆

GARIMA GARG

PENGUIN BOOKS

An imprint of Penguin Random House

PENGUIN BOOKS

USA | Canada | UK | Ireland | Australia
New Zealand | India | South Africa | China

Penguin Books is part of the Penguin Random House group of companies
whose addresses can be found at global.penguinrandomhouse.com

Published by Penguin Random House India Pvt. Ltd
4th Floor, Capital Tower 1, MG Road,
Gurugram 122 002, Haryana, India

Penguin
Random House
India

First published in Penguin Books by Penguin Random House India in 2022

10 9 8 7 6 5 4 3 2 1

ISBN 9780143459040

Typeset by SÜRYA, New Delhi
Printed at Thomson Press India Ltd, New Delhi

www.penguin.co.in

MIX
Paper
FSC FSC® C010615

CONTENTS

Author's Note

During the course of writing this book, I have often received reactions that were on the lines of—but why astrology? Most educated and rational people feel that astrology is, in fact, a relic of our ancestors that doesn't really have a place in the modern world and should be left alone. Until about the latter half of 2019, I would have agreed.

But then I witnessed the rising popularity of astrology in the United States, especially amongst the young and progressive. It was a living paradox because having grown up in India's cosmopolitan New Delhi, it was seen as a superstition. I wanted to understand this huge but interesting gap I had chanced upon. But the more I looked into it, the more astrology revealed itself to me. I began to understand that it was, at its core, a way of understanding our existence in the universe. It was how the ancients made our world a little less terrifying and a little more interesting by storifying the movements of what they saw up above in the night sky and connecting it to what they saw around themselves down here. Astrology, I realised, is not just about the future—it is about the stories of existence, religion, astronomy, culture, psychology and aiding our journeys of self-discovery. My object here is not to convince you, the reader, towards or against astrology in any way but only present a wholly fascinating story that I found hiding in plain sight. I hope you will enjoy tracing the twists and turns of the story of astrology just as much as I have enjoyed putting together this cosmic puzzle.

But how often does it happen that a work becomes a self-fulfilling prophecy? Originally picked up by Westland Publications, the book was nearing its publication when the company was unfortunately shut down. After that, it found its present home in Penguin Random House India. I'm grateful to both companies for their vote of confidence in my work, without which this book wouldn't have become a reality. My literary agent Anish Chandy and editor Karthik Venkatesh not only took a chance on the idea of a first-time author but also helped me navigate the unlikely and fateful ups and downs of this literary journey. I'm grateful to them for giving me the opportunity to write this book and for their constant support, encouragement and grace throughout the two years of this journey. If a book may be judged by its cover, then I'm grateful to Gavin Morris for designing the most beautiful one for this. I'm also grateful to an army of individuals across the editing, design, legal, sales, marketing and other functions because of whom this book has found its way to you.

My research was aided by books, articles, videos and podcasts, but in addition to these, there were also many people who freely gave me their time and insights that have been very helpful—S. Rajmohan, Ankit Pandey, Chris Brennan, Jeffrey Kotyk, Nicholas Campion, Komilla Sutton, Dr. Arjun Pai, Niravta Mathur, Archana Patchirajan, Anton Zvyagintsev and Aswin Subramanyan.

While I have had no formal education or training in astrology, it was in good part because of my maternal aunt, Anu Goyal, who was studying astrology at the time when I began my research that I was better able to appreciate the intricacies of Jyotish. Even though there is no tradition of astrology in my family, in writing this book I have perhaps followed in the spiritual footsteps of my maternal grandfather, Late Ram Swarup Bansal, who enjoyed palmistry and used to love reading the palms of newborn babies in the family. It is also an attempt at uncovering what lies beyond the rational and empirical world—an endeavour I have picked up from my mother, Babita Garg. It is thanks to my brother, Siddharth, that I have learnt to pay attention to detail when writing and developing my ideas beyond the first impulse. Finally, it is because of my father, Ashok Garg, that I have understood the value of working hard which is something I hope I have done with this book.

It is also because of certain events in my life—that took place seemingly out of nowhere and for no reason, i.e., my own fate—that have shaped my reality and ideas of what is possible. Events such as these, which can be both a nightmare or a miracle, have shaped all of our lives since time immemorial and will continue to. *Heavens and Earth*, then, is not only a journalistic investigation into the phenomenon of astrology but also a personal journey into the questions of fate, karma and the nature of life itself.

Prologue: *Story of Astrology*

Once upon a time, a prince of Hastinapur named Dushyant fell in love with Shakuntala, daughter of a revered sage, when he chanced upon her at the hermitage where she lived. They professed their love for each other but their bliss was interrupted when he had to leave, bound by his duty to the throne. He left Shakuntala with his ring which bore the royal insignia and a promise to return. But years passed by and he never showed up. Poor Shakuntala was left so desolate that when a sage showed up, she mistakenly committed the sin of not serving him food, distracted by thoughts of her prince. The incensed sage cursed her that she would be forgotten by the very person she was longing for. But seeing her penitent, the sage relented, and allowed for a way to overcome the curse: she would be remembered again if she showed him proof of their bond.

So she set off on her journey to her prince's kingdom, hoping to be reunited with her lover, her heart full of love and her only proof the ring Dushyant had left behind. On the way, however, the ring slipped from her grasp and fell into a river. She continued her journey with feeble hopes, but the king, predictably, failed to recognise her. But then, fate worked its magic. It just so happened that the ring found its way into the hands of another sage who arrived at the court sometime after a sorrowing Shakuntala had left. In an instant, the ring reminded Dushyant of his time with Shakuntala. At last he reunited with her and their son she had been raising all alone. This son, Bharata, laid the foundation of the Indian civilisation.

Centuries later, Bharata's descendants, the Kauravas and the Pandavas, went up against each other in the great battle for the throne of Hastinapur. But just before the battle, the warrior of warriors, Arjuna, demurred. Why must he kill his own brothers, he asked his charioteer, Lord Krishna. Because in this birth, that is your dharma, or duty, as a warrior and a protector of your clan, he responded. It is only the body that dies and the soul is immortal. In order to fulfil his soul's Karma in that birth, he would have to perform the actions that were in accordance with his dharma, and that was his duty. The consequences of his actions, the deaths of the people he grew up with, of his teachers and elders, were not in his domain to worry about. Whether he chose to fight the battle or not, their fates would unravel. Their lives were not in his control. This dialogue would go on to become one of the most important Hindu texts, known as the

Bhagavad Gita. The bloody battle that ensued ended with the victory of the Pandavas. Following this, the eldest of the Pandavas, Yudhishthira, knelt at the deathbed of Bhishma for advice on how to rule a state. The revered elder talked about many things—free will, destiny and Karma once again. One's Karma was a result of one's good and bad actions in previous lives, he said, and it was only by righteous action that one could thwart the forces of destiny. But as long as one remained in the grip of Karma, it would find one like a calf finds its mother amongst a thousand cows.

The Pandavas went on to rule Hastinapur for years, and when the time came for them to leave it all behind, they renounced their royal lives and proceeded towards afterlife. However, they found that they could not enter Swarga-lok, the Hindu version of heaven, in their Earthly bodies. All except Yudhishthira, the eldest and most righteous of them, perished on the way. But even he could not quite make it. Turns out, he chose not to abandon the stray dog that had followed the family right from the start of their journey when the ruler of Swarga-lok, Lord Indra, told him that the dog could not be taken to the heavenly realm. So steadfast was the prince in his ideals that he chose to go to Naraka-lok, or hell, where the dog could accompany him. But when he got there, he heard the voices of his family and was surprised that they had been taken to hell instead of heaven. It was, however, a test for him. The dog was none other than his own father, Lord of Death and Justice, Yamaraj. He told him that during the great battle, he had been tricked into deceiving a formidable opponent from the Kaurava army, Guru Dronacharya, leading to the latter's death as a result. Yudhishthira, then, had to expiate this Karma before he could truly enjoy his afterlife. Karma, as understood from this story, is not only impossible to avoid, but also invisible at times.

A few generations later, Arjuna's descendants were ensnared in yet another destructive cycle of Karma. King Janamejaya, Arjuna's great-grandson, sought to wreak havoc on all the snakes of the world in a ritual sacrifice, aiming to kill them all, including their ruler, Takshaka. It so happened that the Naga (serpent) king had once played a role in the death of Janamejaya's father, King Parikshit. A few days before his death, Parikshit had insulted a sage who had ignored him by putting a snake around his neck. The sage's son, who watched this, had cursed him to die of a snakebite, and so, when a snake did bite him, Takshaka prevented medical aid from reaching him, to have the curse fulfil its course.

Janamejaya's vengeful sacrifice raged on unabated until a boy sage, Astika, intervened. The son of a Naga mother, he beseeched the king to spare his maternal relations, and thus the cycle of revenge was brought to an end.

In Greece, the three sisters, Moirai, spun the threads of Fate to which both Gods and the mortals had to submit. Clotho held the spindle and fastened the thread for each person, Lachesis measured their lifespan and continued to spin it until their final hour, and finally Atropos stepped in to cut the thread at the appointed hour of death. They were born of Zeus, the king of the Gods; yet even he was not immune to the dictates of the three Fates.

Elsewhere in the world, a Mesopotamian fable of unavoidable destiny has stood the test of time. In 1933, the English writer W. Somerset Maugham retold that story, calling it 'The Appointment in Samarra', where Death itself is the narrator. The story goes like this:

> There was a merchant in Baghdad who sent his servant to market to buy provisions and in a little while the servant came back, white and trembling, and said, 'Master, just now when I was in the marketplace I was jostled by a woman in the crowd and when I turned, I saw it was Death that jostled me. She looked at me and made a threatening gesture. Now, lend me your horse, and I will ride away from this city and avoid my fate. I will go to Samarra and Death will not find me there.' *The merchant lent him his horse, and the servant mounted it, and he dug his spurs in its flanks and as fast as the horse could gallop, he went. Then the merchant went down to the marketplace and he saw me, Death itself, standing in the crowd and he came to me and said,* 'Why did you make a threatening gesture to my servant when you saw him this morning?' *That was not a threatening gesture, I said, it was only a start of surprise. I was astonished to see him in Baghdad, for I had an appointment with him tonight in Samarra.*

These fables of fate lead to some questions. What came first—fate or our active participation in it? Are our lives really subject to delicate and invisible threads that decide our birth, our death and everything that happens in between? Are we totally and completely helpless in the face of our individual destinies? And most importantly, how do we go on about finding the answers to these questions?

Cosmology studies the origin of the universe and everything it includes. For instance, what is the nature of space and where does time come from? We know we are not the centre of our solar system but is the universe so designed that no matter where you stand, you stand at the centre of it? Scientists who study the universe have also found that the core elements that make our life possible—oxygen, carbon, hydrogen, calcium and more—were all formed either as a result of the Big Bang or collisions between stars, billions of years ago, before we arrived on the scene. Even the iron in our blood that courses through our bodies was created out of explosions between supermassive galaxies and nebulae that took place much before. We are, quite literally, stardust. To add on to that, the odds of us being here are quite astronomical as well. As improbable and inexplicable as the event of the Big Bang was, its rate of expansion that gave birth to everything we see up there and down here was just as unlikely.

Stephen Hawking, the celebrated physicist, asked in his book, *A Brief History of Time* (1988), 'Why does the Universe go to all the bother of existing? Is the unified theory so compelling that it brings out its own existence? Or does it need a creator, and if so, does he have any other effect on the Universe? And who created him?' Indeed, *why* does the universe bother to exist? Surely, it's not all so that, as Hawking put it, 'an advanced breed of monkeys on a minor planet of a very average star' could frolic about as they pleased. If there *is* a creator, then towards what purpose have our lives been structured? If there is no creator, then *how* does the universe manage to be so efficiently self-contained? Neuroscience researchers have found that our brain makes decisions a few seconds before we actually become conscious of those decisions, so perhaps something similar takes place at the macrocosmic level as well? In that case, does it dispute our notions of free will?

In other words, it appears that the universe brought itself into existence almost as if by a miracle, our existence is owed to events that took place billions of years before our birth, humans since millennia have observed fate to have an ineluctability to it, and our conscious decisions are not all that subject to what we think is our free will. So, we have to ask the question that most naturally springs to mind here—what on earth is going on and why? It is no wonder that scientists, mathematicians, astronomers, thinkers, and of course, astrologers, have been at it since the advent of human civilisation, for this is a question that can be broached from many different perspectives.

There is perhaps nothing more human than to think about what the future may bring. But while we take these musings for granted today, this impulse was first turned into something meaningful by the ancient astrologer and the stargazer. For them, it began with observing and understanding the patterns of life around us. The sky that was light blue, full of clouds, and held the Sun during the day would be full of stars and the Moon at night. It was almost as if it were alive, then, just like all of us down here. Did it also have a beating heart and a rhythm? Clearly, something was behind the ever-changing sky; and thus began our meaning-making. It was possible, it turned out, to make intuitive connections between what happened up there with what happened down here. It was, at first, a matter of survival for the ancient stargazer. It was important to understand when one might have sunshine and rain so that we could grow our food. It was important to find our way through the stars to navigate the unfathomable darkness of the seas.

This was done by diligently recording the planetary and stellar influences on life around them and drawing conclusions from those, over a period of time. Comets, for instance, signalled the assassination of a king or a prominent administrative figure. Conjunctions of Jupiter and Saturn every twenty years, two of the slowest moving observable planets for the ancient stargazers, heralded societal changes. People born under a certain star were seen as having similar qualities. Patterns so established around the world and since the beginning of civilisation then came to be known as astrology. These were not, and could never be, an exact science, given the immensity and complexity of our existence, but the cyclical repetitiveness of movements up above and their correlation with the events down here had people in thrall. 'As above, so below', the astrologer came to believe.

But were all astrologers the same? Did all of them see the same night sky? Did the stargazers of North America understand the world exactly the same way as those of South America, since the sky looked different for both? If the cosmos was understood by observation, then did the observations of the Hindu astrologer match those of the Greek? How did the Egyptians and the Chinese understand the influence of the Sun and the Moon on our lives? As something that has been around since the advent of human civilisation and intelligence, astrology continued to develop and evolve over time. It seeped into our daily lives, becoming a part of our sciences, philosophies and religions.

But then, somewhere down the line, astrology's younger sibling, astronomy, showed up and had everyone in thrall. It made its older sibling look quirky and eccentric. When there was a lunar eclipse, it told us exactly what happened rather than weave fantastical stories of the fear and change that the eclipse would bring upon our lives. The precision of astronomy seemed to overpower the vagueness of astrology. Also, people had had enough of charlatans and incompetent soothsayers who masqueraded as astrologers and took them for a ride. But did astrology die out entirely? Not really. The lure of the power to tell the future is probably greater still than the claim of a man to being God incarnate. After all, why do we worship if not for the strength to face an uncertain and unknown future? And so, while the practice of astrology became corrupted and continues to remain so for the most part, it did not die. It meandered along, though it had lost most of its sheen.

Why bother with the story of astrology, especially today? We are, after all, highly intelligent self-reliant individuals now and have no need for mythical stories about the cosmos. We can send off space rovers to study the planets and the stars, receiving information from them in real time. Contrast this with, say, the dawn of the sixteenth century, when the Earth was believed to be the centre of the solar system in Europe.

Well, let's consider the astrology and reality of 2020 and 2021 here. According to astrologers, six planets came together in the constellation of Sagittarius in December 2019. In February 2021, there was a similar conjunction in the constellation of Capricorn. Between these fifteen months, we also had a comet and six eclipses. Between May to October in 2021, planets like Saturn, Jupiter and Pluto were in a simultaneous retrograde movement. All of this was just as rare as what happened down here—the Covid-19 pandemic, the world in lockdown, the attacks mounted on the Capitol by a group of embittered Alt-Right activists in the wake of the US presidential election results, the Reddit investors versus the Wall Street fiasco, the surprise takeover of the Taliban in Afghanistan and the wave of protest movements against human rights crises around the world. While astrologers did not predict the particulars of many of these events, it does bear investigation if their correlations have something to them, after all.

But that's just the astrology of the world around us. What about the astrology of the individual? Even if we lack free will, could the movements of Saturn in particular stars and zodiac signs really say anything meaningful about our lives at any given moment? If yes, how do we begin to understand that?

There are millions of details that make up our lives— the place where we are born, the kind of family we grow up in and the emotional and material experiences of our early life that end up leaving a stubborn imprint on the rest of our lives. These determine our sense of right and wrong, aspirations and fears, values and ethics, and more. And then there is that variable that we call our inner voice. In Arjuna's case, it led him to his dharma, which was to fight the war that was waiting for him. But this inner voice, at times, can be something of a wild card. It's not something that dwells in our immediate consciousness, but somewhere deeper—in the reaches of that which we call our soul. Are we born with this variable etched onto our souls or do we develop it in part through the course of our current lives? This is important because it can affect our life in a major way, and yet, it's almost as if it came out of nowhere.

To explain these ambiguities, the Hindu astrologer wove the story of Karma which shows up as fate in our current lives; and for many, fate was bigger than God itself. The Hindus, then, followed Lord Krishna's dictum of performing the actions that life demands of us without worrying about much else. The Greeks believed in amor fati, or the love of one's fate, and stoicism, that is bearing the joys and blows of life with equanimity. These ideas have proved to be enduring because they still have takers.

Our lives often feel accidental in one way or the other. Whether we can ever decisively understand the origin of the universe or fate or not, the presence of chance in our lives is an irrefutable truth that we deal with on a daily basis. It creates uncertainty for us and one often wonders at the unfairness of life. Perhaps that is why astrology is still relevant. It tells us the story of our lives and that of the cosmos in a way that is both rooted and comforting. In these stories, it contains much more that what humans have told each other since the beginning of time, about how they understand the heavenly bodies and the stars. Understanding the story of astrology, then, is about understanding an enduring and ever-evolving human perspective of the cosmos and our place in it.

1

Cosmology: *Stargazers of Yore*

If the movement of the heavenly bodies is an opera show, then astrology is a critic's interpretation of it. But how can we even begin to understand that interpretation if we don't know how the stage is set up? At the very least, we need to know all about the main characters as well as the premise of the plotline to get started. However, for a show of cosmic proportions, it is but natural that one should only get a limited but unique perspective, depending on where they sit. Perhaps a flicker of light brings out the cunning shadows on a character's face; perhaps a song sounds more melodious to those perched on a mezzanine seat and perhaps someone had to take a break and ended up missing a part of the show.

While it is easy to take for granted our knowledge of outer space these days, things were not always so obvious for our ancestors. The ancient stargazers looked up night after night for centuries before they could begin to put together a story of what was going up there. But not all of them saw the night sky in the same way. Some were looking up from the edge of the planet and some were right in the middle of it. And so, every culture around the world interpreted the cosmos with its luminaries in their own way and formulated a cosmology through which they understood the universe as far as they could perceive it. This included their beliefs about how these luminaries affected our lives, how they interacted with each other, and how to worship them. These cosmologies preceded astrological systems everywhere; and to understand the latter, we must understand the former.

Cosmology of the Luminaries

Some of the first human beings to think of themselves in the image of cosmos thought in simple ways. From the stone circles of Neolithic Europe, such as Stonehenge, one could conjecture that early humans were likely able to conceive of a circular solar system and connect it to the cyclicity of life. Indeed, the Triskelion, a popular Celtic symbol first carved into the walls of Newgrange in Ireland shows three interconnected spirals, as if to show the cyclicality of time, space and life. Prehistoric human societies made dedicated spaces to observe the stars, eclipses and summer and winter solstices. Their astronomically aligned monuments, however basic, required significant physical effort to build, and that is possibly the first indication of humanity's deep and eternal preoccupation with the heavens in context of their lives.[1]

The more the earlier humans reflected on life in this way, the more comprehensive their cosmologies became. The Vedic Hindu's wonder about the universe, for instance, can be understood through the 'Nasadiya Sukta' (Hymn of Creation) from the Rig Veda. It starts with the musing that in the beginning there was neither existence nor non-existence, neither day nor night, neither life nor death, but only the One. It ends with a sigh that perhaps the One knows who created the world, but it could be that even the One doesn't know. However, of all that exists, divinity in the form of Brahman or the Ultimate Reality pervades everyone and everything.

In Greece, the birthplace of Western civilisation, the philosopher Plato believed in a geocentric cosmos that emerged out of a single divine creator and hence every single one of its manifestations was divine. The Babylonians, on the other hand, believed that in the beginning there was nothing but water, and all Gods and Goddesses evolved out of it naturally rather than through divine intervention. While the African cosmos was usually gendered with the Sun being masculine and the Moon being feminine, Egyptians worshipped the Goddess Ma'at (the goddess of truth, justice, balance, and most importantly—order), for she was the cosmic order herself. So profound was their sense of alignment with the cosmos that the Great Pyramid, of the three pyramids at Giza, faces north and only deviates by two minutes and twenty-eight seconds from the True North longitude.[2]

The Chinese worshipped the Sun and the Moon as well, but built fewer temples for them. Instead, the main deity was Ti, or Di, or Tian Huang Shang Ti, who was the supreme emperor of heaven.[3] He was associated with the celestial north pole, around which the sky revolved. The Chinese cosmos was, like the imperial state, bureaucratic as the celestial bodies were the court officials of the cosmic state.

The Native Americans believe that in the beginning there was only vast empty space and Tawa, the Sun spirit, and it was the interplay of energies between them that created the world.[4] The Aboriginals of Australia believe that the world was sung into existence[5] and would sometimes even see multiple suns in the sky, which we now understand as parhelia, optical phenomena caused by atmospheric refraction of light.

The underlying belief across most world cosmologies was that of interconnectedness—'as above, so below'. Because of this, our ancestors often sought to mimic cosmic patterns in their daily lives. For instance, astronomers of yore, through approximations of diameters and distances, estimated that you could fit in 108 moons between the Moon and the Earth, and 108 suns between the Sun and Earth. The number then became auspicious and shows up as a significant part of Hindu practices from 108 beads in prayer rosary beads, 108 pressure points in the body in marma ayurvedic massage, and more.

How about the fact that our week is made up of seven luminaries that can be seen with the naked eye? In Roman, Norse and Hindu mythologies, all the days bear similar associations. Sunday, then, is the day of the Sun or Ravi. Monday is the day of the Moon or Soma. Tuesday belongs to the warrior that is Mars, deriving its name from Tiw, who is the pagan God of war and in Hindi, Mangala. Wednesday—Woden's day—is the day of Mercury, i.e., Buddh. Thursday became the day that honoured the mighty Thor or Brihaspati, known as the Guru of the Gods. Friday is the day of Goddess Freya or Shukra, the planet of Venus. Finally, Saturday gets the furthest observable planet of all, which is Saturn or Shani. Each of these planets has a signification that is unique to them, but their overall theme remains consistent across different cultures.

Some of these luminaries were more important than the others. The Sun as the primary source of light was an obvious life-giving force, and so it was worshipped above all. The Aztecs would perform an elaborate ritual to pay their respects to the solar deity. This involved a prisoner of war, chosen to impersonate Tezcatlipoca, God of the night sky. As the living embodiment of a God, he was treated as such and lived in luxury for a year. For twenty days before his eventual sacrifice, the doomed man was allowed to take four women as his wives to represent Aztec Goddesses. Then, on the final day, this man-God was taken to the temple and his beating heart was ripped out of his chest to be offered to the Sun God.[6]

For Sumerians in Mesopotamia, the Sun God Utu

was the 'foe of darkness' who dispensed justice across natural and supernatural realms.[7] For Hindus, he was, and is, Surya, the one who rides a chariot driven by seven horses. In some texts, he also appears in the form of twelve Adityas, each one prominent during a different month of the year. He has several powerful and oft-cited prayers associated with him, from the Aditya Hridyam Strotam to the Gayatri Mantra. In the former he is the power that helps Lord Rama defeat the formidable Ravana; in the latter he is Savitur or the one whose light is the most brilliant of all.

Because it had such life-sustaining properties, human societies have always organised their activities according to its movements. So, when the Sun moves into the constellation of Capricorn from Sagittarius in late December, it is celebrated universally as winter solstice. After this day, the days start becoming longer again after the darkness of cold winter days. This was a time of renewal and rejuvenation as it put normal human life back into motion—agriculture, trade and commerce. Celebrated in the form of many pagan festivals, it morphed into what is now Christmas across the Western world. In India, this celebration takes place in January and is known as Makar Sankranti, where Makar refers to Capricorn and Sankranti refers to the movement of the Sun—also called Uttarayan, the Sun's journey northwards. Across the Indian subcontinent and Southeast Asia, this takes the form of festivals like Lohri, Pongal, Songkran and more. Like the twelve Adityas, there are twelve Sankrantis in a year, with some of them lining up with important regional festivals.

Each of these festivals has been celebrated for thousands of years and will likely be observed for just as long into the future. Many of them are closely tied with regional religious practices and feature elaborate rituals that involve honouring the Sun and nature in some form or the other. It is a testament to the importance of the Sun in our lives that despite our largely secular and modern outlook today, we continue to pay our obeisance to the brilliant yellow star of our solar system.

If the Sun was life-giving, the Moon was evocative. The lone light shone bright and luxuriantly through the blanket of night, along with countless stars. Two major lunar deities were Thoth and Chandra. The former belonged to the Egyptians and the latter is still worshipped by the Hindus. Thoth was depicted as a man with the head of an ibis or a baboon, and considered the inventor of astronomy, astrology, mathematics, geometry, oratory, and more. Chandra in Hindu mythology is a man with twenty-seven wives, each of whom represents the twenty-seven Nakshatras or the lunar mansions in Hindu astronomy and astrology.

The Moon's distinctive waxing and waning was equated with many things in the human realm. A story that is common to cultures from China to Mesoamerica is that of the rabbit and the Moon. This is so because if one looks at the Moon, the dark spots on it seem to resemble a rabbit. Between 600 and 1500 CE, an architectural motif for churches in England's Devon featured three hares, which resembled the Triskelion in its symbolism of cyclicity of life and was also linked to lunar cycles.[8]

It was also found in Buddhist caves in China, where one also finds the story of Jade Rabbit, after which the country named its 2013 Moon rover.[9] In India, this Moon rabbit is referred to as Shashank, which is also a common male name in the country. More universally speaking, lunar influences were, and still are, believed to be the cause of certain mental imbalances, with words like lunatic or loony derived from the Latin word for Moon—'luna'.

The Moon's movements, particularly around the months of February and March, have often marked the start of the new year in many cultures around the world. When winter finally leaves and the warm glow of spring is in the air, the Chinese, Koreans, Japanese, Tibetans and Vietnamese people celebrate their version of the Lunar New Year. The festivities include gathering around with families, eating delicacies and spending the time at home. In India, it's time for harvest festivals as well as the colourful and fun Holi. The dates of the Jewish festival of Rosh Hashanah, which takes place around September according to the Gregorian calendar, are also calculated on the basis of the Moon's movements.

When it came to the five observable planets of Mercury, Venus, Mars, Jupiter and Saturn, their stories were woven around their behaviour and appearances. While Mercury seemed to complete its rotation quickly, Saturn took much longer. So the former became synonymous with quick wit and intelligence, whereas the latter would come to represent delays, coldness and struggle. Venus shone bright and often appeared as a star, and so, most astrological systems would come to consider Venus the significator of luxury and good things in life, including the arts. Jupiter appeared as the largest of all the planets and due to its expansiveness, was believed to bestow wisdom. Finally, Mars, the fiery red planet, became the hot-headed warrior.

These core characteristics then helped these luminaries come alive for us. The characters of this cosmic show acquired greater depth as they became part of local cultures. They were not just mere orbs of light in the night sky anymore; they were Gods, or God-like.

Mercury, for the Mesopotamians, came to be associated with the God Nabu,[10] the scribe and patron of literacy. Saturn, or Shani, became the Hindu God of justice and is still feared for his merciless life lessons. Venus, for the Aztecs, was the patroness of adulterers[11] and for the Chinese, the pale and gloomy planet of war.[12] Jupiter was associated with the chief Babylonian deity, Marduk,[13] the ruler of the cosmos. It was he who created the order of the cosmos, the boundaries of the constellations and the divisions of the year. That made it possible for his subjects to create a calendar through which they could ascertain divine messages and live a life down here that was in harmony with that up in the heavens. The Roman God of war, Mars, was a more benevolent form of the Greek God Ares. The former represented the courage of a warrior rather than the brutality and cruelty of the latter.

But these ancient cosmic Gods were just as flawed as their human worshippers. They had their good qualities but also excesses. It follows, then, that they would also form relationships amongst themselves that would span the range from the bitterest rivalries to the most comforting of friendships.

Venus, for one, only showed up as a star when the Sun was not present, i.e., before sunrise or after sunset. The stargazers concluded that perhaps the two were repelled by each other. And so, this led to the formulation of another astrological principle—a planet's influence is negated when it comes close to the Sun, and this is often Venus for most birth charts. The brilliance of the former burns up everything else. We might understand the myths of Venus's power better by looking at the story of Quetzalcoatl,[14] the Aztec God of winds who is also associated with the planet. When Venus showed up in the sky as the evening star, the God lost vital force and for eight days, he dwelt as one dead in the underworld. But when Venus reappeared as the morning star, the God too went through a rebirth and ascended his divine throne once again. Quetzalcoatl is also known as the feathered serpent, and Aztec iconography portrays a serpent wrapped around his body. This perhaps alludes to the observation that if one were to plot Venus' risings and settings in the sky, it would result in an undulating serpent-like trajectory. The connection between the planet and serpent also shows up in Hinduism's tantric philosophy. Venus is associated with Kundalini Shakti, the enormous power of the serpent of death and rebirth. Even its Sanskrit name, Shukra, refers to the word for male sperm, Shukranu.[15] This further reaffirms Venus' connection to the cycle of life and death, including the rebirth or an awakening that comes after a spiritual or metaphorical death, in both Hindu and Aztec cultures.

Cosmology of Astronomical Phenomena

Heavenly bodies, with their human-like relationships, also underwent the trials and tribulations of such bonds. These were typified through comets and eclipses which were important to map out and understand because they were seen as bad omens that often pointed to disasters. These occurrences, while repetitive, were still infrequent and signified a break from the daily sky movements. That element of uncertainty, especially a potentially harmful one, was a cause for much concern. Eclipses were more common, hiding the Sun at times and the Moon at others.

In Hindu mythology, solar eclipses were believed to have been caused by the demon Svarbhanu, who makes the Sun disappear and wreaks havoc upon the world. It is only after the intervention of the Gods that the Sun is rescued and life is brought back to normal. The Mayans invested so much effort into predicting eclipses that they could calculate the appearance of an eclipse a century in advance.[16]

According to the fourteenth-century French theologian and astrologer, Pierre d'Ailly, an eclipse that came after a Saturn–Jupiter conjunction always led to or coincided with a colossal event such as the fall of Troy, the death of Moses, the foundation of Rome or the advent of Christ. However, astrologers could also go embarrassingly wrong with their interpretation of an eclipse. In 1523, after eclipses preceded a plague in London, people were worried about an upcoming planetary conjunction in which seven planets were coming together in the constellation of Pisces.

Since Pisces is associated with the deep sea, astrologers predicted that a flood of biblical proportions would follow the recent plague. To prepare, people sold off their lands, pitched tents on hilltops and built themselves arks to sail through the water. The flood never happened but that year witnessed the German Peasants' War against aristocratic society. The event was biblical in the sense that it was the most prominent uprising before the French Revolution of 1789, but it wasn't nearly what was predicted.[17]

Comets, because they were much rarer, were feared even more. Several of these were seen during the Mahabharata battle, mentioned in the Bhishma Parva section of the epic. A 'frightful comet' that was seen in the Nakshatra or the lunar asterism of Pushya was said to 'bring about terrible evil to both armies'. Other comets were characterised as 'a white blazing Graha resembling fire emitting smoke' or the 'cruel comet standing between Chitra and Swati, that afflicts both the Sun and the Moon'.[18] Elsewhere too, comets were characterised by their shape, the planets they rose from and the element they represented.

A comet seen in an Earth sign such as Taurus, Virgo and Capricorn foretold a disaster related to the Earth, such as droughts and famine. And so, spotting one in a water sign meant floods, fire signs meant wars, and air signs meant mighty winds and airborne diseases. Because they represented something huge, comets were often bad news for kings and important men of society. It is said that comets were observed around the deaths of Roman emperors Augustus and Constantine the Great as well as the warlord Attila the Hun, among others.[19]

Even literary giants often paid homage to comets. It's not for nothing that in Shakespeare's *Julius Caesar*, a character remarks, 'When beggars die, there are no comets seen; the heavens themselves blaze forth the death of princes.' The Great Comet of 1811, which was believed to have foretold Napoleon's invasion of Russia, was immortalised by Leo Tolstoy in his novel, *War and Peace*. Perhaps, then, it is no surprise that the comet Neowise, which appears once in 6,800 years, made an appearance in 2020. This year of coronavirus and major socio-cultural and political disturbances around the world will be remembered for centuries to come.

Given the timelessness of this cosmic show, its characters, twists and plotlines, it is perhaps not hard to see it as working in patterns or in ever-repeating iterations. Like the cycle of human life and death, it has its cycles too. But since the universe is constantly expanding, these cosmic cycles change their coordinates too. This is where the astronomical phenomenon of precession comes in. The term refers to the change in the rotational axis of a rotating body, in our case, Earth. This can dramatically alter our perception of the night sky. To understand this, we should look at the Pole Star. Every 26,000 years, we get a different star marking Earth's North Pole because of our planet's changing rotational axis, known as the precession of the equinoxes. Polaris or Dhruv Tara is the North Star today, but it used to be Vega or the Abhijit Nakshatra around 12,000 BCE. A little over 3,000 years down the line, the Gamma Cephei star will reign over the North.

But the precession marks an important difference

between the two types of zodiac that are used in astrology—tropical and sidereal. The former, more prevalent in the West, takes the Vernal Equinox or Spring Equinox on March 22 to be its main point of reference for the skies. This is because it relies more on how the seasons change down here on the Earth rather than what is actually going on up there. So, while the Aries sign is supposed to begin from March 22, the Sun actually transits Pisces at that time and only reaches Aries around April 13. The sidereal zodiac, which is the basis of Jyotish (Indian astrology), takes the fixed stars as its main point of reference so as to be more astronomically aligned. Because of axial precession, there is a difference of about 24 degrees between the two zodiacs which reflects in birth charts and their interpretation as well. Where the tropical zodiac will consider one to have an Aries Sun if they are born between March 22 and April 13, the sidereal zodiac will see the individual as a Pisces Sun.

After imprinting his humanity onto the night sky, the ancient stargazer proceeded to write the script of the play. These became the astrological systems that would later guide how everything was going to be interpreted. These astrologies around the world were derived from local cosmologies and included a set of religious rituals, worship and a mimicking of the macrocosm within the microcosm.

Notes

1   Neil Oliver, *Age of Cosmology* (BBC, 2011), https://www.bbc.
     co.uk/programmes/b00z0k23#:~:text=Neil%20Oliver%20
     continues%20his%20journey,very%20idea%20of%20
     Heaven%20itself.
2   Nicholas Campion, *Astrology and Cosmology in the World's
     Religions* (NYU Press, 2012), p. 90.
3   Ibid., p. 99.
4   Ibid., p. 46.
5   Ibid., p. 25.
6   Ibid., p. 65.
7   Ibid., p. 131.
8   *New Scientist*, 'The three hares motif is an ancient mystery
     for our times', 1 April 2016, https://www.newscientist.
     com/article/2082809-the-three-hares-motif-is-an-ancient-
     mystery-for-our-times/.
9   BBC, 'Jade Rabbit: China's Moon Rover Dies', 4 August 2016,
     https://www.bbc.com/news/world-asia-china-36972205.
10   Nicholas Campion, *Astrology and Cosmology in the World's
     Religions* (NYU Press, 2012), p. 132.
11   Ibid., p. 60.
12   Ibid., p. 107.
13   Ibid., p. 128.
14   Ibid., p. 60.
15   Hart Defouw and Robert Svoboda, *Light on Life* (Penguin
     India, 2000), p. 34.
16   Nicholas Campion, *Astrology and Cosmology in the World's
     Religions* (NYU Press, 2012), p. 62.
17   Bobrick Benson, *Fated Sky: Astrology in History* (Simon and
     Schuster, 2006), p. 98.
18   P. V. Kane, *History of Dharmashastra* (Bhandarkar Oriental
     Research Institute, 1962), p. 532.
19   Bobrick Benson, *Fated Sky: Astrology in History* (Simon and
     Schuster, 2006), p. 98.

2

Astrology: *Written in the Stars*

With a cosmological perspective, ancient societies became aware of the changing quality of time. Some moments, they found, were more propitious than others. This meant being in tune with the movements of the Sun, Moon, planets and the stars by facing a certain direction and choosing the right time and day while undertaking an activity. What was auspicious, and what wasn't, was computed after centuries of observing, recording and interpreting data. The patterns so derived were encoded into traditions, stories and calendars, leading to the birth of astrology. In practising astrology, then, the ancients felt they were not mute spectators to life anymore and could exercise at least a degree of free will. For the first time in their uncertain and fragile existence, they felt they could steer their lives howsoever they wanted.

The Mayan civilisation's state priest was known as Ah Kin Mai, or He of the Sun. His job included maintaining the calendars, conducting temple rituals and other official ones, and giving astrological advice to the political elite. As their work involved astronomy and mathematics, they were highly educated and intelligent members of society.

This priest worked on the two Mayan calendars, the Tzolkin and the Haab. The former consisted of thirteen months spread out over 260 days, and was known as the sacred year. The latter, known as the vague year, had eighteen months which totalled up to 365 days. They were observed in tandem with each other and a calendar round, i.e., the time-duration when both coincided, was significant as well. The calendar round would show up after seventy-three sacred years or fifty-two vague years. A month, or uinal, in both calendars lasted for twenty solar days, or kins. These calendars were used to name newborn babies and for a number of religious purposes.[1]

In Mayan astrology, which is still practised, each kin carries a specific quality. It shows the energy of the missions that the human soul is here to undertake and the challenges it will face in doing so. A kin, then, also has an animal, a number and a natural element associated with it. Of the twenty kinds, some are less auspicious than the other. The day of Toj, for instance, is good for bringing what was in dark into light. E, on the other hand, is the day to ask for a woman's hand in marriage or talk to your ancestors because they would be listening on such days. Tzikin, which related to birds, is an excellent day for business and trade.[2]

The Babylonians divided their night sky into eighteen constellations. These included the Pleiades, Orion, Perseus, Auriga and the twelve zodiac-related constellations. While limited initially to the king and the state, Babylonian astrology was later further developed to be applicable to individuals as well. This happened around the fifth century BCE when the sky was pared down to the twelve divisions into the zodiac that we are familiar with today. The compendium of cuneiform tablets, known as the *Enuma Anu Enlil*, recorded during the Assyrian period, is the major source on astrological omens from the region.[3]

The Babylonian calendar was based on the Moon's cycle and the constellation it was found in. So, the major festival of Akitu, or Zagmug, in the first month of Nisan, was timed according to the rising of the first crescent Moon of the year. This festival was much like Easter in which the worshippers recite the *Enuma Elish*, wept over the tragic death of Marduk (the manifestation of Jupiter) and then celebrated his subsequent resurrection.[4] The festival is still celebrated by Assyrians[5] all over the world and its most well-known tradition is Deqna Nissan, which literally translates to Beard of April. For this, decorations of flowers and grass are hung on the door of one's home. So, while the modern-day Babylonians, i.e., Assyrians, may not have Marduk or Jupiter in mind, their celebrations keep the astrological story alive.

In older times, however, those in need of divine

assistance lodged an appeal with the Gods through an astrologer and conducted rituals on the nights of a full or new Moon. These appeals could be quite poetic, such as this one:

> Stand by me, O Gods of the Night!
> Heed my word, O Gods of destinies,
> Anu, Enlil, Ea, and all the great Gods!
> I call to you, Delebat (Venus), Lady of Battles,
> I call to you, O Night, bride of Anu.
> Pleiades, stand on my right,
> Kidney-star, stand on my left!

Anu here refers to the sky as the God of Heavens. Enlil and Ea are his sons, the first of whom is the God of winds and natural forces, and the other rules over Earth and water.[6]

In Egypt, the priest was known as Imy-Wnwt, or the 'hour-watcher'. His duties included timekeeping, calendar collations, conducting purification rituals and 'announcing all the wonders' of the star Sirius. The yearly calendar was designed to foreground the annual event of flooding of the river Nile. For a certain period during the year, the brightest star in the sky, Sirius, would appear so close to the Sun that it would become invisible. Its reappearance as a bright evening star on the eastern horizon would coincide with the flooding of the river in late summer. The flooding restored the fertility of the land and helped facilitate a new cycle of agriculture.[7] It was, in real terms, the beginning of the year for Egyptians.

Priests also played an important role in maintaining Ma'at, the cosmic order. Most temple rituals were devoted to a renewal of creation and order every day. This was done by uttering incantations, making the requisite sacrifices at appropriate times and paying respects to the rising Sun daily—all of which required the priests to have knowledge of astronomy and religion. In this way, the temples were not just prayer houses but served functions of the State. The astrologer–priest helped the rulers defend against unknown hostile forces. The Egyptians also observed their own system of stars, which is known as the Decans. It comprises thirty-six groups of fixed stars and they were in use by European astrologers until as late as the Renaissance.

In the Islamic world, astrology was known as Akham al-Nudium, which translates as 'the decree of the stars'. While orthodox followers of Islam rejected astrology, some offered the alternative interpretation that everything in the world was a way for God to speak to humanity. All natural phenomena, therefore, carried signs from the divine, or ayat. So the religious calendar was based on the movements of the Moon, leading up to the most important festival of Ramadan, and Islamic astrology had its own localised zodiac as well as twenty-eight lunar mansions, known as Al-Manazil.[8]

However, the most enduring astrological legacy from this tradition remained that of Jupiter–Saturn cycles, known as the Great Conjunction. Being the two outermost observable planets, their conjunction represented the cycle of time itself, as they took the longest to meet each other. Everything from plagues to the rise of new kings was seen as a corollary of this conjunction. It takes place every twenty years and foretells a generational change in the world. After twelve such cycles, i.e., 240 years, political upheaval was predicted and after almost a millennium, i.e., 960 years, a new prophet was expected to appear in the world.[9] In December 2020, one such twenty-year conjunction took place, with the planets coming closer to each other than most previous conjunctions. The last time Jupiter and Saturn were this close was in 1623.

When it comes to Chinese astrology, the year-based animal zodiac is often believed to be akin to the Sun sign zodiac—the crucial difference being that where the latter divides the year into twelve parts, the former is a twelve-year cycle where each animal rules an entire year. So, a given year in Chinese zodiac only gives a general indication of what the society at large might expect that year. 2020, for instance, was the year of the Metal Rat, and other such years have seen the Opium War in 1840 and the Great Chinese Famine in 1960. Advanced Chinese astrology goes back thousands of years and is still practised in parts of China. Since the first millennium BCE, astrology in its most intricate form was mostly a function of the state and was prohibited for the general populace for security reasons as it was feared that it could lead to political instability.[10] The chief concern of the astrologer was to establish auspicious times when an undertaking might be successful as well as inauspicious times that should be avoided. Astrology for ordinary people was known as xing ming and a typical reading included the time and date of birth, along with an *I Ching* text, to answer the query at the moment. *I Ching*, or the

Book of Changes, is an important ancient Chinese text, which lays down a system of divination that is practised even today. The text has sixty-four chapters, each of which includes a six-line symbol known as a 'hexagram'. The hexagrams are accompanied with riddle-like verses that can be interpreted to understand what the future holds. Unlike conventional astrological systems, I Ching seems to put the burden of interpretation on the enquirer as only he or she is liable to deconstruct the riddle as it relates to their personal context.

The Chinese system had two lunar mansions, one with twenty-eight constellations which was influenced by the Indian, Persian and Babylonian astrological systems, and another one with about ninety constellations which was indigenous and highly intricate. As in other ancient cultures, there was no distinction between astronomy and astrology, because the interpretation of celestial movements was inseparable from their application to human affairs. This was referred to as tian wen, or sky patterns, and was complemented by calendars known as li fa, or simply, li. The astrological concept, however, was tian xiang, where xiang means an image or a symbol, and the composite word then refers to celestial images or omens. The interpretation of these was further subject to the ideas of yin and yang, which referred to the way in which the energies of the cosmos and the Earth interacted with each other.[11]

While we now take the ethereal names of planets and stars as a given, our solar system didn't always sound so poetic. Before Plato, the Greeks had not allotted names to the planets, but this changed after his student, Philip of Opus, addressed the problem. After that began the tradition of associating their flawed Gods and Goddesses to the planets and developing intricate characterisations for them, which still remains a key feature of astrological literature.[12]

It was in post second century CE Greece that the astrology of the individual, or natal astrology as it is better known, became prevalent for the first time in history. Birth charts were often read in the temples of Serapis, the Greco–Egyptian deity that would later replace the Egyptian God of Osiris in temples during the Roman Empire. One's birth chart was often laid out on a board and the planets were represented by gemstones. These readings included observing the relationships between planets in a birth chart, such as aspects, conjunctions and house lordships, as laid out by astrologers of the time. These relationships were always changing, and that meant some moments were more auspicious than the other. Like today, astrologers back then too fielded questions about life, disease, marriage, wealth, and so on for the most part.[13]

This resonates with India's centuries-old unbroken tradition of astrology. While India has made its way into the twenty-first century as a major geopolitical, cultural and financial power, astrology remains an important part of Indian life. Often known as Vedic astrology, the correct term for it is Jyotish. The term comes from Vedanga Jyotish, which is one of the six parts of the Vedas that form the core philosophical basis of Hinduism.

As it is a Vedanga, or a limb of the Vedas, one cannot gain a complete understanding of the Vedas until one has mastered all Vedangas. Of these, Chandas or meter forms the legs; Kalpa or the art and science of conducting religious rituals is represented by hands; Vyakarana or grammar becomes the face; Nirtukta or etymology is the ears; Shiksha or the correct Sanskrit intonation of chants and prayers is considered to be the human breath and finally, Jyotish or astronomy is believed to be the eyes of the Vedas. This means that it is Jyotish that helps grasp the five other Vedangas and the wisdom of the ancient sages of India in the larger perspective.

Vedanga Jyotish mentions the twenty-seven lunar asterisms, or Nakshatras, and their ruling deities, but it is solely in the context of finding an auspicious time (Muhurta), for conducting a ritual sacrifice, which has been a central Hindu practice since millennia. In this form, the Jyotish of Vedanga Jyotish was primarily cultural, but became the basis of indigenous astrology years down the line. In an astrological context, then, Jyotish is Jyotir Vidya as it is the study of all facets of the 'lords of light': Sun, Moon, planets and stars. The Panchanga is the calendrical system that is used with it. While most Indian calendars are either Sun or Moon based, the Panchanga has five elements that incorporate both solar and lunar markers. These are known as Varana (time-unit day), Nakshatra (lunar asterism), Tithi (phases or days of a lunar month), Karana (half of the Tithi) and Yoga (twenty-seven luni-solar combinations).

Similarities Across Astrological Systems

While each ancient civilisation had its own system of stargazing, one can find many similarities across various astrological systems. For instance, the Moon's nodes are the two points at which its orbit intersects the ecliptic, or Earth's orbit around the Sun. The North node, then, is the ascending node where the Moon moves into the northern ecliptic hemisphere and the South node is the descending node where the Moon moves into the southern ecliptic hemisphere. In Jyotish, this North node is Rahu and the South node is Ketu. They are also understood as the two parts of the disembodied demon Svarbhanu from Hindu mythology.

In Buddhism, Rahula was the son of Gautama Siddhartha, who, at the birth of his son, is believed to have said, '*Rāhulajāto bandhanaṃ jātaṃ*', which translates to 'a rāhu is born, a fetter has arisen'. He was referring to his son being an impediment to his search for enlightenment, which has been taken to mean that children keep one tied into the illusions of the society. That's when the prince decided to leave the royal palace and took the route to become the Buddha upon attaining enlightenment. His son, Rahula, too followed in his father's footsteps and is now revered as an enlightened being. In some depictions, he is shown having a big head, like that of Rahu, and a serpentine lower body, like that of Ketu. From this, we may understand the nature of Rahu and Ketu as complementary—wherever there is a Rahu or a Rahu-like illusion, there is the possibility of enlightenment which is represented by Ketu or the South node of the Moon across astrological systems. In a classical Western context, Rahu and Ketu are also known as the Dragon's Head and the Dragon's Tail respectively.

But these similarities lead to historical research's favourite challenges—dating texts and the flow of knowledge transmission. Since astrology and astronomy were largely indistinguishable until the seventeenth century, the task of following the threads of history becomes a tad more cumbersome. More so in India where knowledge was often transferred orally and many historical records don't even exist. That has frequently made it difficult to establish the provenance of many Indian traditions, astrology in this case, in a way that satisfies Western academia's methods of historical research. Various lively controversies over originality and transmissions across astrological systems have raged, and it is important to discuss them before we move on to the texts and theories.

Western scholars like Indologist William Dwight Whitney and astronomer Jean-Baptiste Biot in the past alleged that Hindus borrowed the lunar asterisms from China or Babylon. To that, P.V. Kane, one of the most prominent Sanskrit scholars and Indologists of the twentieth century, offered, 'If the Nakshatras had been borrowed at one time en bloc from a foreign source, the divergence in the names, in the presiding deities, and in the gender and number should ordinarily not have arisen to the extent they do.'[14] The Nakshatras are not only mentioned in the foundational texts of Hinduism, the Vedas, but in several later astronomical and cultural texts as well. Many of these texts mention a slightly different name for the lunar asterism or a different order in which they should be read. These variations point to an indigenous and organic development of the Nakshatras, according to Kane.

He also asserted that, unlike the rest of the world, the asterisms have always been an intricate part of daily Hindu life. For instance, in the standard Hindu calendar, the months are named after the Nakshatra in which the full Moon appears that month. That is, the first month of Chaitra is named so because the full Moon occurs in the Nakshatra of Chaitra, which falls in the constellation of Virgo, that month. This corresponds to the Gregorian months of April or May and it is during this time that festivals like Chitra Purnima and Chithirai, named after the asterism, have been observed since thousands of years in India.

Transmissions Among Astrological Systems

When it comes to Jyotish, a highly contested piece of the transmission puzzle is the astrological text called the *Yavanajataka*, where Yavana is the Sanskrit word for a Greek person. When Varahamihira, the sixth century Hindu astronomer and astrologer, wrote the *Brihad Jataka*, he mentioned about forty Greek terms in the text.[15] Because the *Brihad Jataka* is one of the five major texts on Hindu predictive astrology, this led many in Western astrological and academic circles to conclude that the modern-day Jyotish was majorly influenced by Hellenistic astrology. This claim was made popular by David Pingree, an American historian of mathematics in the ancient world, when he wrote about the transmission of Hellenistic astrology to India.

Pingree's arguments were based on a single chapter, 'Horavidhih', of the *Yavanajataka* about mathematical astronomy and have since been disproved by various scholars, most recently by Bill Mak, an Indologist at the Needham Research Institute which is affiliated to the University of Cambridge in United Kingdom. In his 2013 paper, titled, 'The Date and Nature of Sphujidhvaja's Yavanajataka Reconsidered in Light of Some Newly Discovered Materials' for the *History of Science in South Asia* journal, he compared the material available to Pingree at the time of his research versus what Mak was able to acquire.

The text, Mak pointed out, was accessed by Pingree in the form of a microfilm of a badly maintained Nepalese manuscript of it, which was in possession of the National Archives of Nepal. On the other hand, Mak accessed it through photos of it taken by another academic in 1954. It turned out to be a much more readable version of the text and had some missing parts as well that Pingree did not have access to.

Mak wrote that works of other scholars had already stated that Pingree's conclusions were 'marred by faulty editing, the incorrect readings being adopted, and the correct ones given in the apparatus criticus, with the result that the translation is incorrect at places and the meaning really intended by the author (of *Yavanajataka*) is lost'.[16] But in addition to that, he also pointed out that the text also mentions concepts like the Nakshatras in the context of military astrology, descriptions of Indian deities, Ayurveda, Karma and more, which are not mentioned in any Greek source at all. So, instead of *Yavanajataka* being the harbinger of astrology to India, he remarks that it was 'most likely conceived in Sanskrit by an author who was conversant in both Greek and Indian astral science, and was certainly greatly familiar with the Indian and the Sanskritic tradition', and so, is an original amalgamation of Greek and Indian astral sciences.

However, Pingree's conclusions, which were published in his PhD dissertation at Harvard University in 1978, continue to be cited even today. But the flimsiness of his conclusion may not be surprising given the fact that one of his advisors was Otto Eduard Neugebauer. The latter, in his work *Exact Sciences in Antiquity*, wrote years prior to Pingree that Indians had borrowed the Muhurtas from Mesopotamians. Given how intrinsic the Muhurtas are to the Vedanga Jyotish and Nakshatras, it was perhaps an even more serious insinuation to make. Kane noted that he had a 'jaundiced' way of looking at all things Indian. He countered Neugebauer's claims with, 'If the writer of the Vedanga Jyotish was a native of the extreme north-west of India or had stayed there for some years he would have easily noticed the difference between the longest day and the shortest day as about twelve ghatikas [because] even illiterate people in the villages of Bombay State know [that].' He went on: 'To suppose that a learned

Indian who was writing a work on Jyotisa had to run all the way from India to Mesopotamia a thousand or more miles for finding out the difference between the longest and shortest day in his own country [...] or for consulting works written in the Cuneiform characters for that purpose almost borders on the absurd.'[17]

Interestingly, Neugebauer was instrumental in the efforts to decipher cuneiform tablets from the Babylonian civilisation. Before that, Western academia insisted that the Babylonians had learnt astrology from the Greeks. The claims were only put to bed when the oldest horoscope ever, dated 29 April 410 BCE, was found in Babylon. Kane wrote about this as well, noting that the transmission was probably the other way round. It was Antiochus I Soter (280-261 BCE) who was instrumental in spreading Babylonian astrology to Greece by introducing it at his school in Kos, a Greek island. In fact, he writes that Ptolemy, the founder of Hellenistic astrology, was of Mesopotamian origin as well, and Indians too were inspired by the Babylonian zodiacal astrology which was later incorporated with the indigenous Nakshatra astrology.[18]

With this, it's easy to see now how delicate the threads of history can be and how liable they are to entanglement. Perhaps these threads can never be unentangled sufficiently as such debates of historicity remain contested in multiple academic fields. But it may be worth remembering that history, after all, is only a particular perspective on past events and not the absolute truth itself. This perspective, in turn, may be shaped by pre-existing power structures and its preoccupations with that particular time and age. And so, the quest to establish where astrology came from and whether the flow of transmission was one way or the other may just be an impossible one. It may never yield certain answers to us because, after all, we're looking into antiquity. But what's more important here is to be mindful of how each major astrological system in the world has had its unique legacy, and for any of these to claim to be the birth of all astrology would be disingenuous at best. It is important to study these systems in their original context because only then can we uncover the unique insights of the astrologer–astronomer that helped build it. To deny, hijack or minimise any astrological perspective, especially for a veiled colonial or a post-colonial project, would be to lose its essence. It would amount to losing the plot of the vastly fascinating cosmic show that is beyond such human politics and divisions.

Notes

1   Nicholas Campion, *Astrology and Cosmology in the World's Religions* (NYU Press, 2012), p. 64.
2   Smithsonian National Museum of the American Indian, The Meaning of the Days in the Maya Sacred Calendar, https:// maya.nmai.si.edu/calendar/calendar-system.
3   Nicholas Campion, *Astrology and Cosmology in the World's Religions* (NYU Press, 2012), p. 124.
4   Ibid., p. 129.
5   Assyrians are native to Iraq, Syria, Turkey and Iran. But there has been emigration and they are found all over the world today.

6   Nicholas Campion, *Astrology and Cosmology in the World's Religions* (NYU Press, 2012), p. 129.

7   Ibid., p. 91.

8   Ibid., p. 177.

9   Ibid., p. 183.

10 Ibid., p. 94.

11 Ibid., p. 102.

12 Ibid., p. 156.

13 Ibid., pp. 157-158.

14 P.V Kane, *History of Dharmashastra* (Bhandarkar Oriental Research Institute, 1962), p. 506

15 Chris Brennan, *The Yavanajataka: Greek Astrology in Sanskrit* (The Astrology Podcast, 2020), https://www.youtube.com/watch?v=D4A0rpK0Dpg.

16 P.V Kane, *History of Dharmashastra* (Bhandarkar Oriental Research Institute, 1962), p. 542

17 Ibid., pp. 549 and 598

18 Ibid.

3

Astrologers: *What Do the Texts Say?*

After astrology came the astrologers. There have been countless unnamed and unsung stargazers who turned to the skies night after night, making observations and documenting their findings. But for an intuitive discipline such as this, it was necessary to bring it all together to make sense of the larger scheme of things. Different astrologers, given their times and intellectual inheritances, focused on different things in different parts of the world. Their astrological efforts were made thousands of years ago but their work can pare everything down to an astronomical occurrence even today—from the Coronavirus pandemic in 2020 to a pimple breaking out on your face. The astrological principles so derived by them are laid down in certain texts, some of which are more widely used than others, and form the basis of modern astrological literature.

Claudius Ptolemy's work has been of significant importance for both Western astrologers and astronomers for much of the Common Era. Born in Ptolemais Hermii, a Greek city in Egypt, in the first century CE, he used to work at the library of Alexandria. Amongst the greatest institutes of learning in the world then, it was at this place that Ptolemy carried out most of his research and work on astronomy, astrology, geography and optics. His most important legacy as an astronomer was to give the Western world a geocentric model of the solar system, according to which Earth was at the centre. As per this model, which would continue to reign supreme well into the sixteenth century, the Sun and the Moon made circular revolutions around the Earth whereas the planets made spiral-like revolutions.

Coming to astrology, however, his seminal work, the *Tetrabiblos*, written in the second century CE, remains relevant even today. It is a four-part text that outlined relationships between planets, characteristics of the planets, the impact of planetary positions on an individual's physical and emotional make-up, and more. He drew from the divination techniques of the Chaldeans, Persians, Egyptians and the Greeks, in composing the text, written in the second century.

Ptolemy began by asking the reader that if farmers and sailors, out of necessity, could use their knowledge of the heavens to steer their efforts towards better fruits, why couldn't one apply the same rules to individual nativities? It tells us something about the timelessness of issues around astrology because he then went on to defend the practice. He wrote that it was often the astrologer's personal incompetence that led to incorrect predictions rather than the inherent premise of the practice itself.

In case of cataclysmic events such as disasters, plagues or wars, he made it clear that it was the national or the regional destiny that dominated, rather than an individual's destiny or natural propensities. But how would one understand the astrology of an event or a country? For this, Ptolemy ascribed astrological placements to all the countries that were known at the time. He divided the world into four parts and each was represented by three zodiac signs.[1]

The first quarter belonged to Europe and included countries like present-day Britain, Germany and Italy among others. These were represented by the fire signs of Aries, Leo and Sagittarius, and ruled by the planets of Mars and Jupiter. According to Ptolemy, 'the natives of these countries are consequently impatient of restraint, lovers of freedom, warlike, industrious, imperious, cleanly and high-minded'. While the Roman Empire saw emperors like Marcus Aurelius during this time, much of Europe was rather provincial and not quite the Jupiterian centre of high learning.

The second quarter included parts of southern Asia, with countries like India, Persia, Babylonia and more. These were ruled by the earth signs of Taurus, Virgo and Capricorn, and the planets of Venus and Saturn. Where

Venus was seen to manifest in Persia where the natives 'wear splendid garments [and ...] fond of elegance and refinement, Saturn afflicted India because people in the country were ill-formed in person, of dirty habits and barbarous manners'.

The third quarter applied to northern Asia and included countries like Armenia, Bactria or the modern-day Afghanistan, Tajikistan and Uzbekistan, and more. These were ruled by the air signs of Gemini, Libra and Aquarius, and the planets of Saturn and Jupiter. So, while the countries here were high on learning, they were also deserted.

The fourth and the final quarter was reserved for countries in the African region. They were represented by the water signs of Cancer, Scorpio and Pisces, and ruled by the planets of Mars and Venus. People here were then both martial and pleasure-loving.

This system was quite basic in formulation, not accounting for the impact of difference in culture, customs and biological features of people in countries even in the same quarter. However, it remains the first known instance of astrology of countries or mundane astrology.

Another notable concept from the *Tetrabiblos* is that of planetary time periods.[2] According to this, different planets rule different stages of an individual's life. The first stage is that of the Moon's and it lasts for four years. In this stage, while one is still a baby, the body lacks fixity and the soul is inarticulate. The next stage, however, lasts for ten years and is ruled by Mercury. This is the time when one learns articulation and develops intelligence. It is the stage of learning about the world and the self.

After this comes Venus, the age of youth. It lasts for eight years and pulls one towards Venusian matters of love and romance. At twenty-four begins the age of the Sun. It lasts for nineteen years and is the longest of all ages. It is the time for an individual to attain maturity, glory and decorum in life. In mid-life, one begins the age of Mars which goes on for fifteen years. It is the age that 'introduces severity and misery into life and implants cares and troubles in the soul and in the body' in order to accomplish something worthy of note. Nearly at old age, one begins the age of Jupiter and it lasts for twelve years. It 'brings out the renunciation of manual labour, toil, turmoil ... and in their place brings foresight, retirement ... he brings men to set store by honour, praise and independence, accompanied by modesty and dignity'. At seventy, one moves into the age of Saturn and it lasts for as long as an individual remains alive. The planet's influence makes the old person 'worn down with age, dispirited, easily offended and hard to please in all situations'. In its division of human life into various parts, this idea is similar to the Vedic idea of ashramas—Brahmacharya, Grihastha, Vanaprastha and Sanyasa.

In addition to these, Ptolemy discussed some conventional ideas as well. These could either be related to the effect of the luminaries on Earth's weather or concepts such as the bodily form and temperament of an individual based on his or her planetary ruler. The universal aspects of life—family relations, marriage, duration of life, one's material fortune and success—were addressed from an astrological perspective. He also wrote about eclipses and comets and how could one make predictions about what they foretold on the basis of their colours and shapes.

When it comes to Islamic astrology, Masha'allah ibn Athari and Abu Ma'shar were two of the most important figures. The former was an Arabic Jew who helped decide the auspicious moment for the founding of the city of Baghdad on 31 July 762 CE. He wrote extensively about astrology and astrolabes, with two of his popular works being *Nativities* and *On Conjunctions, Religions, and People*. The latter, a professor of astrology at Baghdad University in the ninth century, wrote about mathematics of all kinds, including astrological. Eventually, he became the leading Islamic astrologer of his time and set forth his ideas inspired by Persian, Greek and Syriac texts in his work, *The Great Introduction to the Science of Astrology*, which was composed in the year 850 CE.[3] Prominent astrological principles discussed by him include the Great Conjunction, i.e., the conjunction of Jupiter and Saturn, as well as solar returns, both of which are still in vogue amongst astrologers. Incidentally, he also arranged for a translation of Ptolemy's work on astronomy, *Syntaxis Mathematic*, which is better known by its Arabic name, *The Almagest*.[4]

However, a couple of thousand years before these lived Sage Lagadha in India who composed the *Vedanga Jyotish*. While the precise dating of this text is subject to academic debate, some scholars have dated it between 1150 and 1370 BCE based on the astronomical phenomena mentioned in it. The latest possible date for the text is believed to be between 700 and 600 BCE. The text has three recensions where the first belongs to the Rig Veda, the second to the Yajur Veda and the third one known as *Atharvana Jyautisa* is ascribed to the Atharva Veda for the sake of consistency. Written in the form of verses, the former two versions focus on astronomy and are quite similar in terms of content. The third one deals with the Muhurta or what is known as electional astrology today.

The *Vedanga Jyotish* mentions the twenty-seven lunar asterisms as well as their presiding deities. Nakshatras may be classified in many ways based on their observed qualities. So, the Yajur Veda mentions the thirteen asterisms from Krittika to Vishakha as Deva Nakshatras whereas the remaining are considered as Yama Nakshatras. Here, the former were seen as more auspicious and the latter were considered inauspicious. This was relevant for both daily life activities as well as religious sacrifices. In fact, this is something that is reflected in a verse of the Rig Veda recension where the author states, 'The Vedas have indeed been revealed for the sake of the performances of the sacrifices. But these sacrifices are dependent on the various segments of time. Therefore, only he who knows the lore of time, Jyotisa, understands the performance of the sacrifices.' As the text delves extensively into the mathematics of lunar and solar movements as they relate to an hour, day, month and a year, another verse captures the poetry of this knowledge as it says—'Like the combs of the peacocks and the crest-jewels of the serpents, so does the lore of Jyotisa stand at the head of all the lores forming the auxiliaries of the Vedas.'[5]

Interestingly, the Rig Veda recension *Vedanga Jyotish*

does not mention the zodiac signs or Rasi as they are known in Hindi. Unlike astrological texts, it does not assign any astrological meanings or interpretations for the Sun, Moon and the planets as seen in any particular Nakshatra either. In fact, according to scholars T.K.S. Sastry and R. Kochhar, a verse from the Yajur Veda recension which is believed to refer to the zodiac of Pisces has been misinterpreted to be astrological in nature. The duo assert that the Rasis are of a much later origin as well as being of foreign origin and so, their inclusion in modern Jyotish as astrological pointers is a case of assimilation rather than indigenous development.[6]

However, in the later Hindu texts, one can see the evolution of Nakshatras as astrological principles. Each of the Nakshatras is divided into four parts and each is ascribed a unique quality. The asterisms are each associated with a deity from the Hindu mythological canon, a planetary ruler, a sacred mantra known as the 'Beej Mantra', trees and herbs, animals, and more. Moreover, each Nakshatra is associated with a sound or a syllable, which is then used to name a newborn according to his or her Moon Nakshatra even today. While it is not mandatory to do that as a practising Hindu, it is quite prevalent. The principle behind these various associations was to harmonise the frequencies such that the microcosm aligns with the macrocosm.

Jyotish Morphs into Astrology of the Individual

One of the first texts to expand upon Jyotish as the astrological system that we now know was Sage Parashara's *Brihat Parashara Hora Shashtra*, often abbreviated to BPHS. Parashara is believed to have been the grandson of Sage Vasishtha, who was one of the seven main Hindu sages collectively known as the Saptarishi. As with the *Vedanga Jyotish*, it is difficult to decisively establish the antiquity of the text as well as the time when Sage Parashara lived. However, it has been referred to by astrologers for thousands of years and remains the most significant text for the modern-day Jyotish practitioner (Jyotishi) as well. It has been re-interpreted and translated many times over the years, but two of the most commonly available translations are by R. Santhanam and Girish Chand Sharma. The former was published in 1984 and contains ninety-seven chapters, written in the form of over 2,000 verses, whereas the latter was published in 2006. BPHS largely deals with the astrology of the individual, or the native, i.e., natal astrology.

According to the text, there are three components of Jyotish: Hora or divination through the horoscope, Ganita or astronomical placements at the time of birth, and Samhita or reading of omens or body parts like hands. Of these, the text focuses on Hora and discusses the interpretations for different zodiac signs, rising signs, Nakshatras, aspects, the twelve houses, good and bad planetary influences and combinations or Yogas that might be seen in a birth chart.

In Hora astrology, a birth chart is drawn on the basis of one's time, place and date of birth. The birth chart so obtained gives us zodiacal and the Nakshatra placements of the Lagna, or the rising sign, and the Sun, Moon, Moon's nodes Rahu and Ketu and the five planets of Mercury, Venus, Mars, Jupiter and Saturn. After this, we get the Dasha, or the planetary time period. BPHS mentions forty-two different types of Dasha systems, of which Vimshottari Dasha is the most commonly used today. It maps out nine different time periods that total to 120 years. Unlike Ptolemy's system, these 120 years extend to the life of the soul and not one's current incarnation in particular. So one might live out three lives within the span of one cycle of the Vimshottari Dasha or one may live out the entire cycle in one lifetime itself.

Since Jyotish is tied up with the idea of punishments and fruits incurred over many lifetimes, BPHS goes into detail with regard to what different placements can mean for different aspects of a human life right from birth to after death. It spanned all kinds of examples, from premature death and the circumstances of it, what kinds of diseases an individual is vulnerable to at a particular age due to planetary interference, when a person might get married or lose a son or a daughter, what level of professional success one might obtain at a particular age and place, and whether one's soul would travel to heaven, hell, the world of departed ancestors, or simply take birth on Earth again.

After Sage Parashara, the other prolific writer on Jyotish was the astronomer Varahamihira. It is believed that he was the court astrologer of Emperor Chandragupta II around the fifth century CE. He wrote six treatises on the topic, of which the most popular ones today are *Brihad Jataka* and *Brihad Samhita*. Like many today, he bemoaned the hold of astrology amongst common people and felt that the society had forgotten the true meaning of the term 'Hora'. In his conception, he explained, it referred to the fruition of good or bad acts carried out in previous lives. The horoscope, then, was merely a map of how those might compel an individual to live out his or her life in a certain pattern. His was a softer and more nuanced take on astrology, compared to BPHS, which is possibly indicative of the more liberal society in which Varahamihira lived. In fact, at one point, he even remarked, 'If all favourable and unfavourable signs were on one side and on the other side there is purity of heart, it is the latter that brings success.'[7]

He begins *Brihad Jataka,* his work on natal astrology, by writing, '… for the benefit of those broken attempts to cross the ocean of horoscopy, I construct this little boat consisting of a variety of meters with a multiplicity of meanings'.[8] Like many other astrological works, it discusses the interpretations for a variety of planetary and Nakshatra placements. However, it also goes into astonishing detail which we might not even pay heed to or consider relevant enough. For instance, in a group of verses, the author goes into the conditions at the time of a child's birth; location of where the child may be delivered, the direction of the delivery room, direction of the mother's bed, number of midwives or medical staff in the present context, which part of the child's body will be wrapped by the umbilical cord, and more.

Brihat Samhita, on the other hand, pertains to reading of omens and has over hundred chapters. Unlike most astrological works, this one actually goes deep into what makes a good astrologer right from the first chapter.[9] An astrologer must have good hygiene, should be original and imaginative, should not have vices, must not be afflicted with nervousness but should still be meek, and finally, should be a person of remarkable genius. When it comes to learning, the astrologer must know astronomy and should have read the classical texts on the topic. This astrologer must understand the Hindu concept of time which stretches from a Truti, which is 8/13500th of a second, to a Varsha, which is one solar year. It was also vital to know about the various solar and lunar divisions of time. Varahamihira's astrologer also needed to be able to calculate, among other things, the times of the commencement and end of eclipses, the places of the first and last contact, the magnitude and duration of the eclipse and times of the Moon's conjunction with planets as well as other planetary conjunctions.

If one could do all of that and more, then one could proceed towards learning how to read and interpret omens according to the enquirer's personal context. But what kind of omens would you read if you were an astrologer in Varahamihira's time? Well, anything and everything. The cries of birds, the behaviour of cows, horses and elephants; rainbows, dust storms, thunderbolts, comets, meteors; the glow on the horizon, the growth of crops, slits in garments and even pimples.

Known as 'Pitaka Laksana' in Sanskrit, the author's commentary on pimples is quaint at the very least. If a glossy and clear pimple broke out on one's scalp or forehead, it meant one may soon acquire wealth. If this pimple broke out on the crown of one's head, it meant good fortune. But if these pimples sprung up near one's eyebrows, then the opposite was indicated. A pimple on the side of the nose meant great anxiety but one inside the nose may foretell the purchase of clothes. Pimples below one's lips meant one could look forward to good food but if they broke out in one's ears, that indicated a windfall of ornaments, or knowledge of the Atma, or the soul. If one got a pimple on their shoulder, they may wander for alms and cause destruction. In the armpits, the pimples portended acquisition of wealth and comfort. Varahamihira goes on to cover many more events of pimples breaking out in a human body. Pimples, then, are not just the bane of the lives of teenagers and young adults today but had caught the attention of Sage Varahamihira too.

However, lest one think the *Brihat Samhita* is all about ascribing astrological meaning to all manner of trivial human life phenomena, the text goes into astronomy as well. It borrows from the astronomical text of *Surya Siddhanta* as well as Sage Parashara in writing about the four different kinds of planetary conjunctions. These are Bheda, or occultation; Ullekha or near tangential contact; Amsumardana or the grazing of rays and Apasavya or moving apart. Varahamihira gives astrological interpretations of these: a Bheda conjunction of planets may lead to a drought, or influential families of a society may turn on each other. In the Ullekha conjunction, there can be a fear of weapons, rebellion by ministers, and yet, an abundance of good food. In both Amsumardana and Apasavya conjunctions, kings may go to war.[10]

Whether it's Ptolemy's astrological principles or proclamations of Indian sages, a consistent issue with these texts from ancient and medieval times is that they often don't apply to present contexts. So, in older times, if one had an astrological placement that said one would be a rich person, it may have actually been interpreted from a sign that one would have elephants as their vehicle. The same placement today will have to be interpreted in a variety of ways depending on the individual context of the person. For someone born in the crème de la crème of the society, it could mean travelling in a personal jet. And for a villager in a remote part of the world, it may just mean the ability to own a car. In this way, the astrological principles laid down in texts are more of a guide than literal truths and should be understood as such.

Despite the rapid changes in the societal and cultural contexts in which astrology has been received over the years, the texts still remain fundamental to modern-day astrological practice. They reveal much about the times their authors lived in but also serve as documents of historical record. In this way, astrological texts are unique pointers of the preoccupations of the humans that came before us—sometimes connecting us to them, and offering new perspectives on life at other times. But coming to astrology, how did astrologers make use of these texts?

Well, for one, they had to start with measuring the skies. So it was deceptively simple tools devised for the purpose that the ancient stargazer set out to tie a human life to the cosmos.

Notes

1   Ptolemy, *Tetrabiblos* (Davis and Dickson, 1822), Chapter Three in Book Two, https://www.sacred-texts.com/astro/ptb/ptb33.htm.
2   Ibid., Chapter Ten in Book Four, https://www.sacred-texts.com/astro/ptb/ptb73.htm.
3   Abū Maʿšar, eds., Keiji Yamamoto, Charles Burnett and David Pingree, The *Great Introduction to Astrology* (2 vols.), https://brill.com/view/book/edcoll/9789004381230/BP000001.xml.
4   Bobrick Benson, *The Fated Sky: Astrology in History* (Simon and Schuster, 2006), pp. 68-70.
5   Lagadha, *Vedanga Jyotish* (Indian National Science Academy, 1985), https://insa.nic.in/writereaddata/UpLoadedFiles/IJHS/Vol19_3_10_SupplementVedangjyotishaofLagdha.pdf.
6   Lagadha, *Vedanga Jyotish* (Indian National Science Academy, 1985), p. 50.
7   P.V Kane, *History of Dharmashastra* (Bhandarkar Oriental Research Institute, 1962), p. 627.
8   Varahamihira, *Brihad Jataka* (Foster Press, 1885), https://www.wilbourhall.org/pdfs/The_Brihat_Jataka_of_Varaha_Mihira.pdf.
9   Varahamihira, *Brihat Samhita* (South Indian Press, 1884), https://www.wisdomlib.org/hinduism/book/brihat-samhita.
10 Ibid., pp. 185-186.

4

Getting Down to Work:
Tools of the Trade

The project of measuring the skies was both astronomical and astrological. In fact, it was so intertwined that it was hard to distinguish between the two for the most part of human history. While measuring the skies is something we still do, the way the ancients did it was very different. For them, it was not only about knowing the musical notes of the cosmos but also about composing a symphony out of them. In measuring the skies, they started with measuring time. Time was measured at different points during the day, seasons and years, using the simplest of instruments. While for most people that meant one could now have a calendar to manage their lives, for astrologers that meant numerical data could now be ascribed to movements of planets and stars. This data that we now understand as degrees, latitudes and longitudes, was first understood by the astrologer-astronomer in terms of units of time, angles formed by different tools and their shadows, and so on. It is worth understanding the instruments used for these because it shows that astrology did not develop in a vacuum of fantasies and our poetic cosmologies but had a basis in the laws of physics as well.

The first astronomical instruments the world over were ostensibly simple, such as the Indian version of clepsydra or a water clock, the Ghati Yantra. It is mentioned in several ancient astronomical texts of India as well as in the seminal text on administration, *Arthashastra*. Essentially a water clock, it was described as a vessel with a hole at its bottom through which water would flow. The hole was made using a pin, needle, wire or a small rod drawn out of a piece of gold of a particular weight. Time, then, was measured by floating the vessel inside a large receptacle of water and marking the time taken by the vessel to completely sink into water as one ghatika, a unit of time in Hindu astronomy. However, Bhaskara II, the twelfth century astronomer and mathematician, pointed out that it was difficult to construct a vessel and make a hole such that the vessel sank in water exactly sixty times over the span of one day and one night. So his method to correct that was to note the number of times the vessel sank and dividing it by sixty in order to get more precise measurements. Other such tools included nalaka yantra, cakra yantra, dhanur yanta, yasti, and more, which were made out of wood or bamboo. Despite their apparent crudeness, they were well thought out and supplemented by advanced mathematics to not only measure time but also to observe measurements related to the Sun, Moon, planets and the stars.

For the Indian astronomer, however, it was the armillary sphere that was the crowning achievement, according to R.N. Rai's work on Indian astronomical instruments for Indian National Science Academy's *History of Astronomy in India* published in 1985. A variant of it described by Bhaskara II features an elaborate arrangement of a bhagola, the sphere of the fixed stars; khagola, the sphere of the sky beyond the stars and a driggola, the third sphere in which both the bhagola and khagola are united. The instrument looked like a globe and could be used to measure time elapsed since sunrise or the ascendant sign at any given point of time by aligning it to the east direction. But this would only work during the day when the sky was clear. The construction of another novel instrument, that could measure the time and locate the ascendant sign at night, the gola yantra, was described by Aryabhata, one of the most significant mathematicians and astronomers from India, as, 'the sphere which is made of wood, perfectly spherical, uniformly dense all round but light in weight should be made to rotate in keeping with time, with the help of mercury, oil and water and by the application of one's own intellect'.

Elsewhere in Babylonia, in addition to water clocks, hollowed sticks too became some of the earliest astronomical instruments. Daylight was measured by marking out the volume of water flowing from a filled vessel at different times during the day and the year. Alternately, one could note the varying length of a stick's shadow throughout a day and across seasons to get a sense of passing time. These observations were laid down in a cuneiform text known as *Mul.Apin*, named after the star Plough. The text also lists various lists of stars and constellations, periods of visibility of planets, schemes of intercalation of calendars and more for a particular year. While these texts were not known as almanacs at that time, it was precisely that function that they seemed to serve. They not only listed astronomical information but also gave prescriptions for every day of the year.[1] Divided into twelve months, from Nisan to Addaru, each month had thirty days and associated fortunes. So, while the first day of the first month was 'completely favourable', the twenty-eighth day of the ninth month of Kislimu was not a good day for a man to get married. Other days could be unfavourable, bad for bartering grain, primed for revolts and uprisings or destined to bring down the wrath of God. By the seventh century BCE, these almanacs would not only inform people about the upcoming eclipses but their timings as well. Almanacs thus helped put in place the practice of noting down the major dates for significant planetary and stellar movements of the year, making the work of the astrologer–astronomer indispensable to the society at large.

Medieval Astrological Tools: Almanacs, Ephemerides and Astrolabes

Fast forward to 1545 when the first English almanac appeared on the scene. Over the course of the next century, four million copies of over two thousand almanacs would flood the market. At one point, astrological almanacs outsold even the Holy Bible. Another important development at this time was the Western world's shift from a Ptolemaic model, in which Earth was the centre of the solar system, to a Copernican model, in which the Sun was the centre. This shift in the Western astrologer's cosmological worldview was aided by developments in astronomy, and while it reduced the space for astrology, it helped finetune the accuracy of the ephemerides by leaps and bounds. The ephemeris was the more serious version of an almanac, displaying the exact positions in degrees of the Sun, Moon, planets and stars, for a period of many years. It also showed a number of upcoming astronomical phenomena such as eclipses and comets for that duration.

For astrologers, this made their job of casting horoscopes easier, as one now had a lot of astronomical data in one place. One such ephemeris was that of Johannes Stadius, a sixteenth century Flemish mathematician, known as *Ephemerides Novae at Auctae* and published in 1554. This was a significant publication because in addition to listing out the astronomical data, it also explained the apparent retrograde motion of planets for the first time. This work was consulted by astronomers Tycho Brahe and Johannes Kepler as well, both of whom worked on their own ephemeris which would again end up raising the standard for ephemerides for decades to come.

But while almanacs and ephemerides were ready repositories of the latest astronomical data, Islamic astronomy added another variable to the equation. Astrolabes, which were used across the world, were at their peak popularity during the Islamic golden age between the eighth and fourteenth centuries. An astrolabe could be used to measure the altitude of a celestial body above the horizon as well as to chart out the latitude and longitude of a place. In the absence of an almanac or an ephemeris, an astrologer could then use the astrolabe to measure the coordinates and quality of a given moment. He could not only map out the ascendant or rising sign but also the four cardinal points such as the point of the zodiac rising above the eastern horizon, the descendant setting on the western horizon, the point directly overhead and the point diametrically opposite that one. This was followed by dividing the houses and plotting the seven known planets and relevant stars. So, while having an almanac or an ephemeris made an astrologer's work much easier, an astrolabe would suffice for one who knew how to use it.

Astrolabes were also more than just an astronomical and astrological tool. They were also used for religious reasons, such as finding out the exact timings for the daily prayers and locating the direction of Mecca. Many Islamic scholars like Mashallah ibn Athari, Al-Kwarizmi, Al-Beruni and others have written treatises about astrolabes, describing how to use them and their various applications. A notable mention here is Mariam al-Asturlabi, the only female astrolabe maker we know about, according to the History of Science Museum at the University of Oxford. She lived in Syria's Aleppo between 900 and 975 CE and her father, Ijli al-Asturlabi, was also an astrolabe maker. She learned the craft from Muhammad ibn Abd Allah Nastulus or simply, Nastulus. He is credited as being the maker of the oldest surviving astrolabe, which was crafted in 927 or 928 CE and is on display at the Kuwait Museum of Islamic Art.

Since around this time many parts of India were under Islamic rule, the astrolabe made its way to India. The Sultan of Delhi, Firoz Shah Tughlaq, is believed to have ordered the manufacturing of the first astrolabes in India around 1351. The Mughals encouraged the use of astrolabes as a valuable astrological and political tool, with Diya al-Din Muhammad of Lahore producing more than thirty instruments between 1645 and 1680. Not much later, Maharaja Sawai Jai Singh of Jaipur set up an astronomical observatory as well as a centre for manufacturing astrolabes. A Jaipur-made instrument can be distinguished by the fact that they have a plate engraved with twenty-seven degrees upon them, which is the latitude of the city.[2]

A notable mention is the astrolabe ordered by the Maharaja of Patiala in March 1850, likely the only surviving astrolabe in the Gurmukhi script.[3] It was likely made under the instructions of the king's court astrologer, Jyotishi Sri Rishikesh, and all inscriptions on it are in Gurmukhi. It includes a total of six plates that show the latitude and longitude of eleven different cities, including

London, Egypt, Mecca, Patiala, Almora, Delhi, Ayodhya, Lahore and Golconda. The ecliptic on it is divided into twelve signs, with each sign further subdivided into groups of six degrees. The astrolabe also features a total of twenty-two stars, including Nakshatras such Ardra (Betelgeuse), Chitra (Spica) and more, and other stars like Samudra-Paksi (Diphda).

The Astronomer Who Helped Astrology

Of the many great astronomers, Chandrashekhar Samant was the last great naked-eye astronomer in India. He was born on 13 December 1835 to Samanta Syamabandhu Singha, the king of the Khandaparaa state in modern-day Odisha. He is better known as Pathani Samant in his home state, which was a nickname given to him by his family. Initiated into reading the stars by his father, after his formal education ended, he taught himself Lagadha's *Vedanga Jyotish*, Bhaskara II's *Lilavati* and texts on grammar and poetry.[4]

He found himself drawn towards mathematics and astronomy. By the age of fifteen, he started learning about the Lagna, or the ascendant sign, and the method for calculating the ephemeris of planets. Through his own observations, he found that the planets and stars did not appear to be in the positions as predicted by the Hindu astronomical Siddhanta texts. Neither did these texts explain what kind of instruments could be used to make such measurements nor the methods used to arrive at them. So he took it upon himself to correct that gap.

He started working on his own treatise at the age of twenty-six and published it at thirty-four on palm leaves in the Odia script. This work known as *Siddhant Darpana* took another thirty years to be translated into Hindi and printed on paper in the Devanagari script. His greatest achievement, according to his biographers P.C. Naik and L. Satpathy, was that he 'observed, verified, and corrected wherever necessary, all that was known to the Hindu astronomers for thousands of years'.[5] The measurements for the sidereal periods of the Navagrahas and inclinations of the orbits of planets to the ecliptic given by him are almost exactly close to the modern-day measurements. While his work was mostly an expansion of previous astronomical works like the *Surya Siddhanta* and *Siddhanta Siromani*, he had none of the modern-day technology that his contemporaries in the West did. Instead, he devised his own instruments made out of bamboo and wood. Some of these instruments include chapa yantra, mana yantra, his version of gola yantra and a golardha yantra. With these, he could measure local time, altitudes, declination of the Sun and its position along the zodiac belt, height and distance of clouds, the apparent retrograde motion of planets, mean motion of planets to correctly determine their position in the sky, latitudes and longitudes of planets, and more.

His work has been so enduring that even today one of the major Hindu temples, Jagannath Puri, still employs his astronomical calculations to calculate Muhurtas for religious purposes. His home state, Odisha, has a planetarium named after him as well as a museum dedicated to him. But where Samant was focused on astronomy, there were many stargazers in India who focused only on astrology. Their astrology was rooted not just in the planets and the stars but in concepts of space and time as well. Their astrology, then, was their grand model of human life itself.

Notes

1   Khalid Salim Isma'el and A.R. George, *Tablets From The Sippar Library* (Cambridge University Press, 2014), Chapter Eleven, https://eprints.soas.ac.uk/1621/2/tablets_from_the_sippar_library_xi_the_babylonian_almanac.pdf.

2   V.N. Sharma, *Sawai Jai Singh and His Astronomy* (Motilal Banarasidass, 2016), https://books.google.nl/books?id=QRA2mgZnXXMC&printsec=frontcover&hl=en&source=gbs_v2_summary_r#v=onepage&q&f=false.

3   S.R. Sarma, *The Gurmukhi Astrolabe of the Maharaja of Patiala* (Indian Journal of History of Science, 2012), https://srsarma.in/pdf/articles/2012_Gurmukhi_Astrolabe.pdf.

4   P.C Naik and L. Satpathy, *Samanta Chandra Shekhar* (Bulletin of Astronomical Society of India, 1998), http://articles.adsabs.harvard.edu//full/1998BASI...26...33N/0000033.000.html.

5   Ibid.

5

Deep Dive into Indian Astrology:
Shining a Light on Jyotish

How exactly did Jyotish transform from a system of calculating Muhurtas into a discipline that mapped the fate of individuals? What was it that inspired sages Parashara, Varahamihira and countless others to write their texts and for those who came after them to remain connected to the skies? Jyotish thrives even today in a way that is unlike its many global counterparts. But why exactly?

The ancient Hindu, among other things, was thoroughly spellbound by the world up above and around. So much so that Kala, or Time itself, became something of a deity.

It existed without a physicality to it and seemed to go on forever. It could be an Anu or two atoms of time, a Nimesha or the time it takes to wink or a Paksha, which is a fortnight. Time could also be measured by the life of Brahma, the God of creation and the fourteen realms of existence in Hindu thought. A day in Brahma's life is Kalpa, in which the realms of existence pass through different kinds of societies, flooding over, rejuvenation and other processes of creation and destruction, for over four billion years. The night of Brahma lasts just as long, and in this, ten realms of existence meet their complete dissolution. This can also be understood as the 'Lila', the cosmic dance and play. It goes on endlessly in cycles and in the *Bhagavad Gita*, Lord Krishna who assumes the form of the supreme God akin to the Brahman described it thus:

> At the end of the night of time all things return to my
>   nature;
> and when the new day of time begins, I bring them again
>   into light.
> Thus, through my nature I bring forth all creation and
> this rolls around in the circles of time.
> But I am not bound by this vast work of creation. I am
> and I watch the drama of works.
> I watch and in its work of creation nature brings forth all
> that moves and moves not
> and thus, the revolutions of the world go round.[1]

But even beyond this Kalpa wherein we play our parts in the cosmic Lila, there is Mahapralaya, lasting for over 300 trillion years, in which all fourteen realms of existence are destroyed. Time could then be contracted to the minutest and expanded beyond the conceivable limits of the human mind. Somewhere in this endless space–time continuum of multiple universes, our Navagrahas and the Nakshatras perform their great show. Countless souls abound in this existence, with their dance flowing into many lifetimes. Interpreting the rhythms of this dance in tandem with the cosmic show is Jyotish.

The Jyotishi, or the one who practices Jyotish, in ancient India started out by finding a way to align the microcosm with the macrocosm. This was the practice of calculating a Muhurta for it, i.e., the auspicious timing to conduct a religious ritual or undertake an activity. But years down the line, it developed into what we now understand as astrology. The astrological principles were laid down in texts as we saw previously and could be studied under a learned person or a sage. This astrologer, then, could not only calculate the Muhurtas but also interpret a variety of natural phenomena and read an individual birth chart to predict the future.

Becoming a Jyotishi, however, was no simple task. Traditionally, one was initiated into the discipline if the teacher deemed a student worthy enough. Once initiated, the student was instructed orally and through texts in Sanskrit. To be a true master, one had to memorise the texts by daily repetition, which was complemented by the teacher's commentary. In doing so, it was believed one would come to embody the very spirit of Jyotir Vidya, or the knowledge of astrology. Another reason was that it was believed that with proper pronunciation, Sanskrit spoke to the very soul of living creatures. And so, in order to truly understand and gauge the essence of Vedas, it is still believed that one must read them in Sanskrit. One of the first things the Jyotishi began learning was Samkhya philosophy.[2]

Jyotish and Samkhya Philosophy

According to Samkhya, one of the six main schools of Hindu thought, the universe is composed of various elements or Tattvas. Of these Tattvas, Purusha is the only one that is constant and unchangeable. It is the consciousness, which transcends time, space and causation. All that exists, including you and me, does so because Purusha desired to experience itself. That inspired Prakriti, matter or nature, to manifest itself into reality that can be perceived. While Purusha and Prakriti are often mistranslated as male and female energies, it is important to remember that both of these transcend the constructs of gender.

However, there is a duality to them and the awareness of this dualistic existence is Buddhi, the limitless awareness. The individuation of the Buddhi is Ahamkara, ego, in simple terms. It is Ahamkara that makes an individual think that one is performing an action or experiencing an emotion. This self-identification finally becomes the basis of the law of Karma.

Ahamkara can be experienced in three ways, or mediated by three Gunas. These are the Sattva, Tamas, and Rajas. Of these, Sattva is the individuality that is relatively self-aware of its true nature. It gives rise to Manas, mind and the ten senses. These include the five senses of perception which are hearing, touch, sight, taste and smell, through which information flows from the external to the internal. The other five are senses of action that are speech (symbolising verbalisation of thought), hands (symbolising creative action), feet (symbolising an ability to move), genitals (reproduction) and anus (symbolising elimination of waste from the body). In this, the flow is directed from the internal to the external.

The next Guna is Tamas, which is the organic individual that is relatively unaware of the self's nature. It represents the five senses of sound, texture, form, flavour and odour. Combining these, we get the 'Pancha Mahabhutas', or the five great elements, of ether, air, fire, water and Earth. Finally, there is Rajas, the middle ground between Sattva and Tamas. It is the ability to become relatively more or less self-aware. It does not produce anything of its own but is an interplay of what Sattva and Tamas experience.

The Buddhi is believed to be Sattvic in nature. The Manas, senses and the body are believed to be Tamasic in an ascending order. The Ahamkara is understood to be Rajasic. This means that one can steer one's ego experience to greater self-awareness using one's Buddhi by losing identification with the Manas, senses and the body. Finally, one's soul is beyond these classifications. Theoretically, the Gunas can exist in an absolute form. However, each individual has a unique composition of these three qualities and their expression is constantly fluctuating in ourselves. These fluctuations often lead to imbalances and there are many ways in which that might show up.

But what does all of this have to do with astrology? Well, one's rising or ascendant sign represents the nature of one's Ahamkara. One's moon sign or the moon Nakshatra shows how one's Manas will experience this Ahamkara. The sun sign is one's Atma or the soul that observes the current life as it is experienced by the individual. Lastly, the placement of one's Mercury will show how one uses the intellect, or Buddhi, to navigate this experience and observation. The actions so performed by one become one's Karma.

The law of Karma is relevant beyond astrology and there are many schools of thought on it even outside Hinduism. In its hipster or New Age conception, it is understood as cosmic vengeance of sorts. However, it is at the same time simpler and more complex than that. Perhaps it helps to look at it as something similar to Newton's Third Law of Motion where for every action, there is an equal and opposite reaction. If you are charitable, you are shown charity in return. But say your act of charity was to donate food to the poor, that you purchased from a local shop. There are a number of possibilities as to what may have happened to that food before it arrived at the shop. Maybe the land on which it was grown was unjustly acquired and so whatever is produced on it is tainted somehow. Or maybe the middleman did not pay a fair price to the farmer or the factory worker who produced that food. Or maybe the shop-owner was unscrupulous. In any of these cases, you are becoming an unwitting agent of Karma by transferring the taint associated with that food to the final consumer. It might end up affecting you adversely if the

Karma associated is heavy or it may pass by unnoticed if not.

The reason behind this strange simplicity and complexity is that the law of Karma operates eternally. Everyone who is living out their life on Earth at the moment is tied up in limitless and incomprehensible threads of Karma. It is not only our soul that has lived out many, many lifetimes but also those of people around us—our families, friends, strangers. Even if one lives the life of a saint in a current lifetime, one will still have to bear the consequences of what one did in past lifetimes and this may be borne out by interactions with other people. The Karmic ledger, then, is like a double-entry book accounting, where debits and credits have to be balanced out before one can get out of the game.

Where does this Karma come from? It became active the moment Prakriti emerged as a result of Purusha's desire. It was the primordial action that led to a ripple of other actions that have and will go on creating their own ripples till the end of oceanic time, which might very well be endless. The only way to escape this process for an individual soul is to attain Moksha, or the ultimate liberation. This comes after one's Karmic ledger has been balanced out and the soul has no more desires left, including the desire to not have any desires. At this point, a soul manages to transcend the world of cause and effect and liberates itself from Time itself. The true aim of a Jyotishi is to help an individual get in alignment with this process of attaining Moksha by apprising an individual of their Karmas, so that the person can begin to live a life that will help more in exhausting past Karma than creating new Karma.

In Jyotish's framework, Karma is divided into four categories. It can be Sanchita, the collection of all Karmas of a soul. It can be Prarabdha or the Karmas that act upon us in a current lifetime. It can be Kriyamana or the Karma we create in the current lifetime out of free will. And finally, it can be Agama, which are the Karmas that one will experience in future lifetimes. An individual experiences these Karmas according to one's make-up of Gunas and their impact on one's astrologically determined Ahamkara, Manas, Atma and Buddhi. When one has more Sattvic qualities, one is not attached to the results of their efforts. On the other hand, when one is more Rajasic, one is driven by desires and acts out of passion. Tamasic tendencies mean one is reactive or thoughtless and acts without quite realising why one is doing something.[3]

So, it might be one's destiny to become a Bollywood superstar. That would be her Sanchita Karma. But at what point in her life she will become one will be determined by her Prarabdha Karma. She may be a child actor or she might regale her audience from her youth until the old age. In either case, how she handles her fame would be important because that will become a part of her Kriyamana Karma. Does she let the fame get to her head? Or does she understand the fleetingness of it and stay rooted? This is important because this may be the only part of our existence that is relatively in our control. Our psychological response to life and our consequent actions may be Sattvic, Tamasic or Rajasic. Whichever way she gravitates, it will become her Agama Karma and she will experience the consequences of it in her future lifetimes.

But let's say she is not happy with her life and wants to cosmically engineer her way into or out of a situation. While it can be done, a lot depends on the intensity of one's Karma. These intensities are of three kinds. The first of these is Dridha, or completely fixed. This is the kind of Karma that cannot be mitigated at all. So, if it was her Dridha Karma to become a superstar, there is no way she could have avoided it. Think of Rekha, the veteran Bollywood superstar, who appeared in her first movie at the age of thirteen. She has recounted in her interviews how tough the experience was and how much she wanted to be in school at the time, rather than act in movies. But because it was probably her fixed Karma, it was not up to her. However, some Karmas may be a little flexible and they are termed as Dridha–Adridha, or fixed and non-fixed. Here, one can alleviate the experience of one's fixed destiny by putting in considerable effort. And then, there are Adridha Karmas, which are non-fixed and easily mitigated. At the same time, mitigation of one's Karma to any extent doesn't imply that one can escape it. Whatever the quality and intensity of it, one needs self-awareness and conscious action to lessen its impact. For this reason, suicide is frowned upon in many cultures, including Hinduism. Without a body, the soul become unable to live out its Karmas and may suffer as a result.

The Five Kinds of Jyotish

But when it comes to reading a birth chart, it may be done in more ways than one. There are five major systems of Jyotish—Parashari, Nadi, Jaimini, Tantric and Tajik. Each of these branches have their own astrological texts and a system of practice, making them unique in character.[4]

Parashari Jyotish, as we saw previously, was developed by Sage Parashara. However, a lot of what is now understood as Parashari Jyotish was developed by unknown astrologers. Successive generations of astrologers would develop their own astrological principles based on their practice but would share those with the public under the name of Sage Parashara in order to be taken seriously. Varahamihira was instrumental in helping develop this particular system. Other important works of Parashari Jyotish that are still relevant are *Saravali*, *Jataka Parijata* and *Phaladipika*.

Nadi Jyotish's origin is hard to pinpoint, much like the Parashari system. However, it is one of the most fascinating systems of all. Legend has it that at some point, the Hindu sages worked out the science of Jyotish so well that they were able to write horoscopes for people who were not even born yet. These horoscopes were more formulaic and so, could be applicable over many centuries. Written by various authors over time, there are primarily four collections of such horoscopes—*Bhrigu Nadi*, *Parashara Nadi*, *Shuka Nadi* and *Chandra Nadi*. The horoscopes today remain in the custody of families of astrologers who have a tradition of astrology going back generations.

These families or astrological lineages guard these Nadis as a treasure. It is believed that a person visits a particular Nadi astrologer if their horoscope already exists with the said astrologer; in other words, it is destined. If one cannot find theirs, then it is either lost or one has not yet found the right Nadi Jyotishi to visit. Nadi readings are consulted for predictions related to general issues like marriage, career and finance, as well as one's past life Karma.

Jaimini Jyotish is another popular form of astrology practised today. It was developed by Sage Jaimini and was further expanded upon by astrologers down the line. While it varies from the Parashari system quite a lot, it does borrow some elements from it. Today, astrologers often use techniques from both systems in their readings.

Tantric Jyotish is an evasive form of Jyotish, whose origins are almost impossible to establish. Tantra is the mystical form of Hindu thought that is believed to be an offshoot of the Atharva Veda, one of the four Vedic texts. Of the techniques employed by this form of astrology, some can be rather mysterious. Defouw and Svoboda list some of these in their book, *Light on Life*, such as the observation and interpretation of omens, the Jyotishi's breathing patterns at the moment a question is asked, client's speech-patterns and actions and past life readings, among others. This form of Jyotish is not practised widely and it is hard for an average person to seek out someone for a reading.

Tajika Jyotish gets its name from the Sanskrit word for an Arab, Tajik. It is also known as Neelakantha Tajika after its main proponent, Neelakantha Daivajna, who was a sixteenth century scholar and the court astrologer of the Mughal emperor Akbar. This system deals with astrological results for a whole year, also known as Varshaphal. This is the concept of solar return, i.e., the time during a year when the Sun returns to the same longitudinal degree as at the birth of the individual. Based on this, a horoscope, known as Varsha-Kundli, is created and is then read for predictions. Other aspects of this form of Jyotish include Arabic astrological techniques such as reading the sextile, square, trine and opposition, which can be found in Ptolemaic astrology as well.

In addition to these systems of Jyotish, astrologers may also employ non-astrological divination techniques such as Sankhya Shastra or numerology, Samudrika Shashtra or divination by reading body parts, using their shapes, relative size and markings, and Hasta Samudrika Shastra or palmistry.

While learning from a teacher and reading the texts may give one an intellectual understanding of astrology, Jyotishis are expected to understand the world around them better than most people. For this reason, the study of Jyotish was traditionally accompanied by the study of Ayurveda, or the Hindu science of medicine and food, Niti Shastra, or political science, Yoga, and Vedanta philosophy to name a few disciplines. Over time, elements from a variety of such disciplines have become so intricately connected with astrological principles that it can be hard to tell where astrology ends and non-astrology begins.

For instance, the Samkhya principle of Gunas can

be applied in Ayurveda. Sattvic foods are those that are directly derived from nature, and these include fresh fruits, vegetables, nuts and whole grains. Rajasic foods are those that include processing such as preserved food, alcohol and caffeine, fried and salted food, and more. Tamasic food, in addition to much of what is Rajasic, represents the excessive intake of fats and sugar, meat and more. In the same way, the Ayurvedic theory of bodily constitutions, or Doshas, can be used astrologically as well. The Doshas, namely Vata, Pitta and Kapha roughly translate as wind, bile and phlegm. Here Vata is the body's air and ether elements, Pitta is fire and water elements and Kapha is water and Earth elements. Saturn governs Vata, the Sun and Mars govern Pitta, Jupiter governs Kapha, the Moon and Venus govern both Vata and Kapha, and Mercury governs all three. So, on the one hand, an Ayurvedic practitioner may help alleviate problems of one's Dosha by looking at the client's Gunas, on the other hand the astrologer may help balance one's Gunas by prescribing remedies on the basis of one's Dosha.[5]

These remedies are known as Upaya in Hindi and are supposed to help with the mitigation of one's Karma. They are usually something simple like chanting a particular sacred mantra, visiting a temple, donating milk and so on. More esoterically-inclined Jyotishis may suggest wearing a particular gemstone or consuming a certain herb. All of these are dependent on one's Grahas and the energies one is trying to synthesise or harmonise. For a remedy to work, it must meet certain parameters. The astrologer must diagnose the problem accurately, must be spiritually neutral, the remedy must be appropriate, and the Muhurta accompanying it must favour its success. However, many Jyotishis completely eschew such remedies and prefer to counsel their clients only on an emotional and mental level.

But whether a Jyotishi believes in remedies or not, one is expected to be highly attuned to the cosmos. This is why it is often referred to as a Sadhana or a spiritual practice. For traditional Jyotishis, this means daily worship of one's Ishta Devata or one's personal deity and performing Homa or a religious ritual. Others may simply meditate upon the teachings of their chosen teachers or gurus, whether or not one has formally studied under them. In either case, there has to be an element of self-transcendence and devotion to something higher. One reason for this is that without this, one cannot be free of vested interests and his or her own subconscious prejudices, biases and more. Attempting to overcome this is the first step towards reading a chart correctly and within the right context. But there is a deeper reason for that as well—the belief that mystical knowledge of Jyotish can only be attained by becoming one with it. Meditating on the planets, stars, their significations, first-hand information from reading birth charts and so on help them go beyond the texts. With this, they can come upon their own unique insights that they can apply to their practice. In fact, this is important for the survival of Jyotish itself because without this, it will fail to adapt to the changing mores of society.

This reflection is how Jyotishis of the past came to

associate a variety of different things in the world around us with a Graha or a Nakshatra. For them, there is an underlying interconnectedness to a particular vibration that may radiate from the macrocosmic to the microcosmic level. So, Grahas and Nakshatras have associations such as geographical directions, places, flowers and trees, diseases, emotional temperaments, colours, clothes, professions, body parts, bodily substances, distances, flavours, geometrical shapes, direction of glance, heights, metals and gems, methods of persuasion, psychological states, family relations, seasons, gender and caste.[6] In the present context, it is not uncommon to hear astrologers associate technology with Rahu as the Graha is associated with electricity. Specifically, it is supposed to represent the technology that features some kind of an illusion. So, Rahu is often associated with social media and photography since both have the power to create an illusion which is the domain of this Graha.

In this way, there are three levels at which a Jyotishi operates—reading the technicalities of a birth chart, applying one's mind in understanding the context of it and finally, using one's intuition as guided by Sadhana to receive astrological insights for the chart.

Jyotish in Indian Society

While today anyone can practise Jyotish, traditionally there were certain communities who were given the task of performing astrological tasks. These include the Joshis (derived from Jyotishi), Kerala's Ganaka and Kaniyar and

Orissa's Abadhana, among others. Their tasks included preparing the Panchanga, announcing key Panchanga dates in villages, reading and matching horoscopes, and more. This ensured a certain continuity of practice at even the most basic level of the society. However, the assimilation of Jyotish with daily life in India goes deeper than that.

Where a vast majority of Hindus do not understand intricacies of Jyotish and Karma, they are exposed to Jyotish from an early age. Newborn babies are often named according to the syllables of their birth star, or Janma Nakshatra, whether the family believes in astrology or not. Honouring one's departed ancestors is considered quite important as well, and failure to conduct the appropriate rituals and prayers at the point of cremation can invite the Pitri Dosha to one's birth chart. If it shows up in one's chart in a current lifetime, then it means that someone in one's paternal lineage was not cremated properly and it will manifest as delays and issues in one's quotidian activities. Since we owe our biological life to our ancestors, a failure to give them a proper departure from the earthly world will add to our Karmas and will show up in our consecutive lifetimes. Even during the days of Shraadh, which come before the festival of Deepavali, one honours one's departed ancestors by feeding food to crows or making donations. In these days, one is not supposed to make significant purchases and will not be able to find a Muhurta to conduct a Hindu wedding ceremony.

Apart from this, movies and shows too play an important role, reiterating the themes of astrology in Indian society.

Many Bollywood movies feature the motif of Karma and reincarnation prominently—*Karz* (1980), *Kudrat*, (1981), and more recently, *Om Shanti Om* (2007). All of these movies had the main protagonist remembering a past life where they were murdered, and seeking justice in their current avatar. *What's Your Rashee* (2009) had the male protagonist meet twelve women, one from each zodiac sign (all essayed by Priyanka Chopra-Jonas), to find a suitable woman for marriage. Many Indian movies and shows also feature a Jyotishi and birth charts as a motif, especially for scenes involving a Hindu wedding. Because of this, even a non-religious and culturally uprooted Indian will have a certain awareness of life that fits in with the mould of Jyotish.

Hindus often consult astrologers for a variety of major and daily life decisions such as finding out the auspicious time to move into a new home, matching of horoscopes before fixing a wedding and the auspicious time to hold the ceremony, undertaking a new professional venture, making a financial investment, legal affairs, and so on. For most people throughout history, the preferred Jyotishi was either the local temple priest or someone in the extended family who dabbled in astrology out of interest. The reason behind this was that one should not make one's living through Jyotish as this was viewed as something that would inevitably corrupt one's astrology. After all, if someone visits an astrologer wanting to know if they'll ever gain material success or live abroad and their chart does not show combinations for the same, the client might just refuse to pay for the consultation. If one's bread and butter depends on such consultations, one is liable to twist facts and inevitably mislead the client.

Yet, when India reformed its private sector in the early 1990s, it led to massive commercialisation of Jyotish, both offline and online. What was supposed to be a spiritual practice was now officially a big business. Today, one can find a Jyotishi at every nook and corner. Of course, the vast majority of these are not honest and skilled practitioners, at least not if we view them from the perspective of ancient Jyotishis. While there have always been crooks who have misused people's belief in astrology to make money out of it, there is now a thriving market full of such Jyotishis that harm more than help. They give out motivated astrological diagnoses and sell highly-priced remedial solutions to their clients. This has led to superstition and ignorance amongst people who continue to visit such astrologers, which is disastrous for society overall. Such a practice of Jyotish has also ruined many lives with terms like Manglik Dosha, Rahu-Ketu and Sade Sati thrown around as if they are the end of one's life. At the same time, this has caused much disrepute to the knowledge of Jyotish as well.

However, as the Indian consumer matures, many have begun to seek out astrologers whose credibility can be vouched for, even if they offer services at premium prices. This modern Jyotishi is much like a therapist, who acts as a confidante and a counsellor for her clients trying to navigate the uncertain waters of life. This makes it extremely important to find the right Jyotishi, much like one would settle on a therapist they feel comfortable with.

Whether one ever seeks out a Jyotishi or an astrologer or not, it can be interesting to understand what a birth chart truly is and what it represents. It is, after all, a snapshot of the movie of epic proportions that our soul is witnessing in the cosmic vastness.

Notes

1   Fritjof Capra, *The Tao of Physics* (Flamingo Harper Collins Publishers, 1983), p. 220.
2   Hart Defouw and Robert Svoboda, *Light on Life* (Penguin India, 2000), pp. 50-51.
3   Ibid., Chapter Two.
4   Ibid., Chapter One.
5   Ibid., p. 139.
6   Ibid., Chapter Five.

6

The Birth Chart:
Anatomy of the Kundli and Navagrahas

The birth chart is the main document of an astrological activity, including Jyotish. Astronomically, it shows the positions of the Sun, Moon, planets and the stars for any given time, date and the latitude-longitude of the place of birth. Astrologically, it shows the quality of time itself at the time of your birth. Judging the quality of this time is the task of the astrologer, for which one relies not only on astrological literature of yore but also on personal skill. Different astrological systems across the world use varying techniques for mapping the birth chart, and in Jyotish, there are broadly three styles—North Indian,

South Indian and East Indian. All astrological charts, Western or Jyotish, will tell a similar story of an individual, but with different flavours. So, while there are the same twelve signs and houses everywhere, they are interpreted differently by astrologers according to their particular tradition.

In Jyotish, the birth chart or the Kundli as it is known in Hindi is a map of a soul's life so far and perhaps its future as well. The soul is the size of a thumb and has been around for countless lifetimes, taking on different bodies in different parts of the world at different points of time. In this sense, it has had a life of its own and has performed various acts of love, service, jealousy and anger, and indulged in ill-considered or thoughtless actions throughout its journey. Each of these acts has led to an equal and opposite reaction which we experience in the current lifetime. This remains relevant even in the case of twins and co-borns as each of their souls will tell a unique story but there will obviously be some overlap.

In other words, the birth chart explains the phenomena of the 'accident of birth'—why we are born in a certain family, experience certain emotions and feelings, events in our life, and so on. Of course, many never feel the need to explore the accidents of their life, and for them, the promise of astrology is practically non-existent. But for even the most rational mind, it is discomfiting to look at the instance of birth as a zero or a neutral starting point. After all, factors preceding our birth such as our parents and their individual contexts influence our lives just as much as our own experiences. While all astrological systems seek to relate the story of our lives with the planetary and stellar bodies, Jyotish relates it to the factors of time and space as well, by incorporating the concepts of reincarnation and Karma. Our current life, then, is not as much of an accident as we might like to think, and the Kundli is the first gateway to understand that.

However, as prevalent and sought-after astrology is in India, even the most ardent enquirer will not know the intricacies of Jyotish or a Kundli. Most Indians simply want to know their future through this medium, maximising their material gains and minimising their life challenges. That puts power in the hands of the astrologer, who might or might not have the client's best interests at heart. But even when they do, they might not have the skills to adequately grasp the great chasm between the possibilities and the realities of a particular birth chart.

Since a birth chart is a lot more than what might happen in future, it is perhaps useful to understand what it represents on the whole. The chart shows the degree-wise placements of one's planets in particular houses and signs. A Kundli, unlike other birth charts, is a repository of not just one chart for an individual but several divisional charts known as Vargas.

The main chart, however, remains the same across different astrological systems. This chart shows one's ascendant sign, or Lagna in Hindi. This Lagna can be any of the twelve constellations that was rising on the eastern horizon during the event of one's birth. Since these change every two hours and sometimes even quicker, it is believed to be a reliable indicator of one's ego self or

Ahamkara. While it's hard to see how a certain animal became associated with a particular zodiac sign, the associations are now fairly universal and interpretations are made in accordance with them. Each system does it in their way and so does Jyotish. It describes the journey of soul from the first sign, Aries, to the last, Pisces, across countless lifetimes.

Understanding the Zodiac

Each sign represents a particular station of the soul in a current lifetime and so, one's Lagna immediately gives some information about one's mission in this life. Here, the names of the signs in Hindi refer to the symbol or the animal with which that sign is associated.

Aries, or Mesha in Hindi, represents the primordial birth of life itself. It is the sign of creation, impulse and adventure, all of which are necessary to manifest life as we know it. For this reason, Aries is the beginning of a new cycle for a soul. This means that whatever the soul has learnt in the past lifetimes may not be of much use in the current one as it now starts on a new cycle of awareness. The sign is represented by the ram, which, like the Aries individual, is quick to butt heads with its rivals.

It follows, then, that Taurus, or Vrishabha, is the building of a foundation after that first impulse of Aries. For this reason, it is also the most fixed sign of the zodiac. The soul must build a strong and fixed foundation here, helping life perpetuate itself. It is represented by Lord Shiva's bull, Nandi, and is often worshipped by married women for begetting a child, since reproduction keeps the society going. It could also be said that it is the birth of a child that gives a couple the Taurean foundation to their marriage.

In Gemini, or Mithuna, intellect and communication are born after life has been comfortably established in Taurus. The soul here revels in the pleasures of the mind so much so that the sign is represented as twins or a man and a woman, which shows the duality of thought that is natural to people here. Here the soul can think in multiple modes, in terms of male–female, order–chaos, spiritual–material, and so on.

Then Cancer, or Karkata, is when one starts to nurture new projects after one has thought through what one wants in Gemini. In both the Western and Indian astrological systems, it is represented by the crab. The marine animal has a hard outer shell but a soft underbelly and can also survive on land. At this point, the soul might still be living in an intellectual and emotional world but it wades into the practicalities of real life as well, gradually. In other words, it attempts to come out of its shell.

But Leo, or Simha, is where the soul is confident to come out and shine in the world after the experiences of Cancer. Represented by the lion, it wants to show itself off to everyone and owns its sense of being regal. For this reason, people with Leo tend to be in the limelight more than any other sign.

For a Virgo, or Kanya, however, the soul seeks perfection after it has grown weary of the adulation of Leo. It wants to even out all imperfections of life and reach the heights of completeness in doing so. But since life remains imperfect as ever, the soul here invariably deals with much disappointment and discomfort. It is understood as the Virgin, embodying a purity or perfection of sorts.

So, when it comes to Libra, or Tula, the soul tries to let go of the Virgo's need for perfection and instead tries to strike a balance between the material and the spiritual. The life for a Libra person, then, is a constant struggle between two opposite ends where one never quite manages to be at peace. Just like the balance scale, it is actually never balanced as long as it has something material to deal with.

It is with Scorpio, or Vrishchika, that the soul begins its ascent towards the spiritual leaving the material behind with Libra. Represented by the scorpion that lives in the desert, the soul starves itself of the superficial and is quite intense here. It is the soul's first true dive into the occult and unknown mysteries of existence. But no matter how hard it tries, it doesn't manage to uncover everything that it wants.

With Sagittarius, or Dhanu, the soul realises that it was still in the throes of the material in Scorpio. So this is where it begins to dissociate itself with the body and that is why the sign is often represented as a half centaur and half man. It begins to shed its animalistic instincts and move towards the spiritual in the earnest through the wisdom gained by learning and knowledge.

With Capricorn, or Makara, then, the soul tries to take on as many challenges as possible to speed up the road to enlightenment it started with Sagittarius. The sign is associated with Saturn, the planet of Karma, and so people with a prominent Capricorn may have very Karmic or difficult lives. The soul here deliberately makes things difficult for itself in order to exhaust its Karma, so that it may move to the next step. So while the soul is trying to move towards the height of spirituality, it cannot do so until it has dealt with the material in its toughest forms. Where as in Western astrology it is represented by the Babylonian sea goat,* in Jyotish it is a sea dragon. Either way, it is emblematic of chaos and the resulting wisdom.

After the harshness of Capricorn comes Aquarius, or Kumbha. Here the soul seeks to go beyond itself, and the sign is associated with the practice of Kumbhaka, which is about breath control. The breath, or the Prana, is the beginning and end of everything, and so controlling it helps one master a spiritual form of existence. The sign also represents large social networks, which means that people in this placement believe in giving more than taking. It is universally represented as a man or a woman holding a pot of water, which refers to its giving and volunteer-like sacrificial qualities.

Finally, we come to Pisces, or Meena, where one attains spiritual liberation. Here the soul completes the cycle of awareness it began in Aries and now has fully moved beyond it. Throughout this long process, it has gone through multiple ego-deaths to lose identification with the material and immerse itself into nothingness of the cosmos. It will, however, in the next birth begin a new

---

*Contrary to popular belief, it was originally a sea goat and not a mountain goat. 'Capricornus (The Sea Goat)', https://chandra.harvard.edu/photo/constellations/capricornus.html.

or a higher cycle of awareness and will go through similar challenges as it did in this cycle. It is often represented as fishes going in a circular direction, not just alluding to the oceanic nature of the sign but a sense of completion too.

The Lagna, as one's main sign, also represents the first house in the chart. But there are eleven other signs and houses too. So, what do they signify? Each of these houses represents other aspects of one's life, receiving guidance from their Lagna, or the ego self. The ascendant decides which sign is going to rule which house for an individual—so Venus might rule relationships for one sign and career for the other. That is important because even though the planet has certain qualities associated with it, those will manifest differently for different ascendants based on the houses they rule. But even if two people have the same ascendant, the same planet might be placed in two different houses. That will greatly alter how they experience that specific aspect in their life.

Let's break this down further. Each of the houses sequentially carries the energy of the zodiac, so the first house is a lot like Aries, the second is like Taurus, and so on. After one has understood the self in the first house, the second house shows one's family and wealth much like Taurus. The third house, then, like Gemini, represents one's communications, but also one's siblings, friends and short-distance travels. In the fourth house, which represents one's mother and early home environment, a person's nurture is highlighted. Like Cancer, it is where one was comfortable but was also preparing for life ahead. In the fifth house, as with Leo, one learns about one's creations—whether they are artistic, romantic or biological. In the sixth house, as with Virgo, one faces bitter experiences in the form of one's enemies and the realities of daily living.

In the seventh house, like Libra, one strikes a balance between the self and others. It is the house of one's personal and professional relationships. Moving on to the eighth house, one sees where one's Scorpio-like intensity will be focused on in this lifetime, and what one could unearth only to be transformed by it. With the ninth house, then, one can understand where one's greatest gains of wisdom and higher learning would occur. While it could be literal academic or religious learning for many, it could also come through relationships or children depending on the sign and the planet placed here. It is also the house of good luck in the chart. Next up is the house of discipline and hardships of Capricorn, i.e., the tenth house. It shows where one would work the hardest and the highest status one would reach in life. In the era of social and professional networking, the eleventh house or the house of Aquarius becomes all the more important. So, if one struggles with this aspect of modern life or is especially good at it, one may want to explore one's eleventh house. Finally, we come to the twelfth house, which, like Pisces, indicates where we attain our liberation and release. It is the house furthest away from the house of self, so here one literally escapes the self through the pleasures of the bed, intoxicants and spirituality. People who move significantly far away from their place of birth tend to have important placements here.

Once we have figured out the undercurrent of one's chart with the Lagna, signs and houses, it's time to understand the Grahas themselves. Literally translated as 'energy-seizers', a Graha is believed to impact an individual by catching hold of certain energies in the universe. Unless one becomes conscious of the influence of one's Grahas and begins to transcend them by turning spiritual, one subconsciously submits to these influences.

Understanding the Navagrahas

The most important Graha in Jyotish is not the Sun but the Moon, or Chandra, since it is our actual mind, or Manas. It represents our subconscious and unconscious, shaping our most immediate and natural reactions to life. Since every other aspect of our life is coloured by these reactions, it follows that it should reign supreme in the reading of a birth chart. As the Moon is constantly waxing, waning and showing up in a different constellation every other day, it represents the changeability of the human mind. Since our minds are significantly shaped by our early life, Chandra also represents the motherly nurturing we experienced while growing up and how that coloured our view of the world.

Next up is the Sun, or Surya. It is our soul, or Atma, and wherever the brilliance of the Graha shines in a chart is where one's soul feels most aligned with its true purpose. But because it's so good at this one particular aspect, the Graha here also shows where one might be excessively proud. It is the Graha of authority figures in our lives, including our father, because that's how we usually gain a practical sense of the world as opposed to the emotional or lunar influence of the mother.

Since our lives are heavily dictated by our Karmic influences, the next two important Grahas are Rahu and Ketu. Unlike others, they are not actual planets but merely astronomical points where the orbits of Surya and Chandra intersect. The northern intersection, then, is Rahu and the southern intersection is Ketu. These are also known as lunar nodes and their story is derived from the Samudra Manthan myth. When the great churning yielded the Amrit, the nectar of immortality, it was being distributed amongst the Devas, or the celestial beings. However, the Asuras, the non-celestial beings, wanted some of it too. One of these, Svarbhanu, managed to disguise himself as a Deva and found his way to the place where the Amrit was being distributed. He had just had a drop of it when Surya and Chandra noticed that something was amiss. They raised an alarm, and at this Lord Vishnu instantly cut off the head of this Asura and the Amrit never reached the body. The head of this Asura became Rahu and its headless body became Ketu.

While this story elucidates the perpetual enmity that Rahu and Ketu have towards the Sun and Moon, which is why they cause eclipses every now and then, it also tells us what Rahu and Ketu are as Grahas. Where the Graha of Rahu constantly hungers for Amrit and believes it has obtained it, the Graha of Ketu feels perpetually lost without the head and the Amrit. The former represents one's hungry illusions in one's current life; the latter represents the area of life that one is detached from. The tussle of one's Manas and Atma is dictated by the churning caused between one's Rahu and Ketu.

Next up, we have the five observable planets. While the influence of the Grahas above tends more to the subconscious and is out of our conscious control, the remaining ones are more future-oriented influences and dictate aspects of our life that we build on ourselves.

The stories of Mercury and Jupiter are entwined. The latter, Brihaspati, was much absorbed in learning and rituals, as one would expect, being the teacher of the Gods themselves. His wife, Tara, was left alone and found herself enchanted by the sensuous and promiscuous Chandra. The two had a passionate encounter and ended up conceiving a child. When the teacher, or Guru, found out about the child, instead of blaming the couple or confronting his own negligence to his wife, he cursed the unborn child to take birth as one of neuter gender. Mercury, or Buddh, was that child and this duality is captured in one of the signs it rules, Gemini. So where one's Guru might show one's wisdom as well as what one might neglect, one's Buddh or Buddhi will represent one's intellect as well as duality.

The Graha of Venus, or Shukra, shows where one derives aesthetic and material pleasure from. It is ruled by Shukracharya, the teacher of Asuras, and while it indicates what can give oodles of pleasure, it does not guarantee true happiness. The Graha of Mars, or Mangala, gives one courage and the will to take action. It is ruled by Lord Shiva's celibate son, Kartikeya, who was born to vanquish a demon called Taraka. The manner of his birth is a story of celestial trickery but ultimately, the seven-day-old infant still managed to kill the demon. So, where Shukra shows what might keep us in the realm of material happiness, Mangala shows where we might find our courage and aggression.

Finally, there is the Graha of Saturn, or Shani. Furthest away from the Sun and lonesome, it has themes of fear, rejection and hardships associated with it. Indeed, the story associated with it helps understand just that. Surya, with his brilliance, tired out his wife, Sandhya, and she left. When he went looking for her, he found Chhaya, her shadow and twin sister. He conceived a child with her but when he realised the mix-up, in godly fashion, instead of owning up to his mistake, he rejected both Chhaya and the child, Shani. The child, then, grew up feeling rejected by the authority figure that was his biological father, Surya, and was nurtured by the shadow of a mother. This illustrates that wherever the Graha is placed in a chart, one feels unfairly treated and it is usually the most difficult aspect of one's life.

Each of these nine Grahas also cast their glances on various houses, in addition to the houses where they are placed and the houses they rule. These glances, or Drishtis, are known as aspects and are a common feature in many astrological systems. At times, a house may have more than one Graha situated in it, and that forms what is known as a conjunction. In these conjunctions, one sees the power play of the Grahas, as the more powerful ones will weaken the softer ones. So, if one has the Sun and Saturn conjunct anywhere in a chart, it might be an especially challenging aspect for one, as the two Grahas don't like each other and may create discomfort.

Reading the Kundli

Now that we have understood the influences in a chart, it's time to figure out what happens when. While a chart may hint at a lot, only a fraction of it will ever come true or bear fruit. One of the reasons for that is the concept of planetary time periods, or the Dasha. As we saw previously, there are over forty such time period systems, but the most commonly used one is the Vimshottari Dasha system. It literally translates into 'direction of 120 years'. While it follows a certain sequence, not everyone lives out the same dashas at the same points in life, unlike the Ptolemaic system, since it is the soul's 120-year journey and not the current body's. So, if you died at the end of Saturn's time period in your last lifetime, you must have begun the current one with Mercury's time period, as it comes next in sequence. These time periods dictate which Graha will play an important role in your life at a given time. So if you are currently running the time period of Venus, then not only will Venusian themes feature prominently in your life but your particular experience of Venus will also come alive. That means the sign, the house, the Nakshatra and the aspects and conjunctions related to it will come alive for you, based on how Venus is placed in your birth chart.

Each planet has a particular associated time period and these are unevenly distributed in length. So, while the Sun's period lasts for six years, the period of Venus is twenty years long. These time periods are also subject to when they take place in a current life—a Venus Dasha would induce your marriage if it occurs between the ages of fifteen to thirty-five, but it's unlikely it would lead to the same result if it ran from your birth up to the age of twenty.

But this was just about one's Lagna chart. If one wanted to zoom into a particular aspect of life, one would look at the Varga charts. These are divisions of the main chart itself and give a much deeper look into that specific aspect of one's life. So, if one were to zoom into the ninth house of good luck, one would get the Navamsha chart. After the Lagna and Moon chart, it is the most frequently consulted chart because it relates to marriage. In a country of arranged marriages, one definitely wants to consult the cosmos for future prospects.

By this point, we can see why reading a birth chart or a Kundli is a seriously complicated affair. That puts a question mark on the mass consumption of astrology in India. In addition to how an enquirer usually knows next to nothing about their chart or Jyotish, most people also remain ignorant of a crucial factor. An average Jyotishi will only have the bare minimum knowledge and skill to see what may happen, as opposed to what will happen. This Jyotishi resembles the general practitioner who will write out a quick prescription for the common ailments that form the bulk of his or her practice. But if that flu is a symptom of a much serious problem, one will have to visit a specialised doctor. In a similar way, one's experience of

Jyotish can be greatly affected by what sort of Jyotishi one chooses to consult.

At the same time, while an astrologer may judge a birth chart or a placement to be good or bad, the cosmos itself is indifferent. It is not out to get anyone in particular and it does not favour some over others. So, an astrologer might see an unstable career in your birth chart, but for you it might just allude to your freelancing gig that you do, in fact, enjoy. Or the astrologer may foretell difficulties for a woman with placements that show her to be a strong individual because at the times the texts were written only men were supposed to go out in the world and women were supposed to stay at home or be involved in activities that engaged their nurturing instincts. But for a woman living in the twenty-first century, it probably works out for the better for her to be more outgoing and assertive.

To take major life decisions based on astrological advice, especially from an average Jyotishi, would be something that not even sages Parashara or Varahamihira would recommend. But even if one were to participate in an astrological venture, not just the astrologer, even the client should be aware of the gravity and complexity of the task. Whether one uses Jyotish for self-realisation or to improve their material life, they need to remind themselves that this spiritual discipline has often been seen to be evasive with answers. So, whatever one gets out of it must not be taken as gospel truth and one's own intellect, intuition and faith should be one's North Star rather than even the best of astrological skills.

But where believers are quick to cede the agency of

their future to an astrologer, sceptics are eager to reject an alternative worldview based on their limited experience and knowledge of Jyotish and astrology. Astrology is one of the many perspectives on the nature of life, among other things. Other than our general temperaments, life events and the world in general, astrology lets us look at the story of our lives from a unique vantage point. It can tell us about the possibilities and limitations of our individual lives but it can also give us insights into our psyche. In Jyotish, this can be done by exploring the stories of lunar asterisms or Nakshatras.

7

Personifying the Stars:
Stories of Nakshatras and Other Stars

If we are stardust, can the stars really say something about what goes on in our minds? And if that is possible, then which omniscient stars are we to consult? There are one septillion stars in our universe, give or take. That's one followed by twenty-four zeroes. Of these, some 400 billion are part of our little corner of the Milky Way galaxy. But from wherever you stand on our planet, you can see a maximum of only 2,500 stars at a time. Of these, most of us can only recognise the Orion, Ursa Major, and the North Star. Every other twinkling light for us is just that, a twinkling light.

However, the ancient astronomer–astrologer had a greater appetite for imagination and storytelling than we do today. The stars, like the Sun and the Moon and the planets, appeared to move. Their apparent randomness yielded to patterns of shapes that were familiar to humans, which is where our twelve-part zodiac came from. So, while the stars of Aries might not look anything like the ram to us, that is how the ancients decided to codify that bunch of stars in order to pass on its stories to the rest of humanity to come. And thus began the theatre of stars.

Unlike other luminaries, individual stars did not have a personality of their own. But taken in a group, they were capable of telling poignant stories. The cluster of Seven Sisters, for instance, is one of the most visible in the night sky and has been storified in cultures across the world. For the Greeks, these stars told the story of Pleiades, the seven companions of the Greek Goddess of hunting, Artemis. Orion, the ruthless hunter, fell for the youngest of these sisters, Merope. He raped her and pursued her mercilessly as she tried to escape. Zeus, the God of sky, interfered and froze that chase for eternity by turning the seven sisters and the hunter into stars. So, even though the three stars that form the belt of Orion point to the Pleiades, he can never really reach them. Hindus, on the other hand, wove the story of Krittikas around the cluster. There are several versions of the same story but essentially, it involves the seven sages or Saptarishi, their wives and the fire God Agni. Agni wanted a union with all the seven wives. While some accounts say he raped six of them, others say he was tricked by his admirer, Svaha, daughter of Sage

Daksha, who impersonated the women, desirous of union with him. But in every version of this story, the seventh of these wives, Arundhati, escaped unhurt because of her purity and chastity. The six wives, on the other hand, were so overcome with shame that they took refuge in the heavens, and they represent the stars of the Seven Sisters. In both the Greek and the Hindu stories of these stars, then, we see the timeless tale of a woman's battle for her dignity etched onto the night sky forever.

This is where the story of the Nakshatras begins, for stories such as those of the Krittikas were not mere mythologies. For one, they help identify the clusters and constellations quickly. You need not draw out a map of the night sky or be an astronomer to find the Seven Sisters if you can spot the three stars that form the belt of Orion. But astrologically, they contain an encyclopaedia's worth of information. Krittika, which lies in the constellation of Taurus, is one of the twenty-seven Nakshatras or lunar asterisms in Jyotish. In addition, there exists the twenty-eighth Nakshatra of Abhijit, but it is not considered for modern-day astrological and religious purposes.

While the stories of the Nakshatras were woven centuries ago, they are still relevant, as Jyotish is intimately connected to Hindu mythology and the essence of the Krittika Nakshatra lies in its story as well. Like the six wives, people born in this asterism can cut ties with this world or earthly pleasures and elevate themselves to the heavens or a higher spiritual plane. Like Agni, they can be interested in other people's partners. Like Arundhati, they can be pure or have the ability to purify themselves through transformative events in their life. In fact, the chastity and devotion of Arundhati was such that even today, a newly-wed couple in South India is shown the stars of Arundhati and her husband Vashishth to imbue these ideals in their new life. Astronomically, these are the stars of Mizar and Alcor that lie in the Ursa Major.

The essential meanings of all Nakshatras date back to Vedic times when any kind of a ritual was undertaken according to the moment's auspiciousness for it. In other words, was the quality of the time conducive to the activity being undertaken? That a relationship existed between the stars and the activities undertaken down here was a matter of years of observation and record-keeping. Krittika, then, was not considered auspicious for wedding rituals as the Nakshatra was observed to be associated with the abrupt interruption of matters. The story of Krittika, like all astrological stories across the world, was a way to encode the quality of the time that is represented by the asterism in a way that could easily be passed on. It is much easier and impactful to tell the story of the six Krittikas, Agni, Svaha and Arundhati, than it would be to pass on a dry analysis of astronomical data.

Nakshatras in Daily Hindu Life

Even before astrology was imbued with this cultural astronomy, Nakshatras were embedded into the daily life of Indians. As we saw before, each of the months in the Hindu calendar derive their name from the asterism in which the full Moon occurs that month, so the first month becomes Chaitra because of the full Moon in the Nakshatra of Chitra. The following months, then, are Vaishaka (Vishaka Nakshatra), Jyaistha (Jyeshtha), Ashadha (Purva Ashadha or Uttara Ashadha), Sravana (Shravan), Bhadra (Purva Bhadra or Uttara Bhadra), Asvina (Ashwin), Kartika (Krittika), Agrahayana (Mrigashira), Pausa (Pushya), Magha (Magha), and finally, Phalguna (Purva Phalguni or Uttara Phalguni). The Purva and Uttara Nakshatras here are understood as pairs, where Purva means former and Uttara is latter. So, in the month of Bhadra, the Moon may be seen in either the Purva Bhadra or the Uttara Bhadra Nakshatra.

Many festivals and religious rituals were dated according to full Moon appearances in certain Nakshatras. These include Thaipoosam, which is related to the Nakshatra of Pushya and is celebrated wherever one finds a sizeable Tamil population in both India and outside. Another festival is Kartik Poornima that takes place around late October or November and is related to the Nakshatra of Krittika. The most popular celebration of this festival takes place in Varanasi, the holiest of places for Hindus, and is known as Dev Deepawali or the Deepawali of the Gods. Thousands of devotees throng the steps by the Ganges to take a dip and pay homage to their departed ancestors. In many ways, it is a new year for Hindus. A month later the Ardra Darisanam takes place in the south of India, which is related to the Nakshatra of Ardra. These festivals have been celebrated in the subcontinent for thousands of years and form an important part of the modern-day cultural life in the region as well. Many of the temples across the subcontinent tend to have a corner dedicated to the Nakshatras or the deity Naksatrani. In Tamil Nadu, there are twenty-seven temples, with one that corresponds to each of the twenty-seven Nakshatras. Spread out across the state, one can visit the temple associated with one's asterism and perform the relevant ritual prayer.

P.V. Kane also outlines references from *Taittiriya Samhita*, which dates back to 300–400 BCE at the minimum, to show how the lunar asterisms were connected to agriculture and seasonal changes. So, Ardra became associated with teardrops because when the Sun appeared in it, rains would set in. Similarly, the next one in the order, Punarvasu, was linked to rejuvenation or renewal because at this point, the crops sown at the field would begin to sprout to life. After this, the crops would need to be nourished regularly in order for them to grow, and because the Sun would be seen in Pushya, the asterism would then come to be associated with nourishment. Ashlesha gets its symbolism of clinginess from the crops of paddy and barley embracing each other, whereas Magha represents finality of this agricultural wealth in the form of the crop harvest.[1] The twenty-seven asterisms have been mentioned in various other Hindu texts, along with the stars that are supposed to represent them and their ruling deities. The Nakshatras were often characterised by their intrinsic qualities such as being constructive or destructive, fixed or movable, and so on. These qualities led to the formulation of rules, which were then applied to all domains of daily life such as marriage, the consecration of a deity's idol in a temple, construction of a new house, entering that house for the first time, shaving facial hair, birth of a child, and much more.

The text *Hiranyakesigrihya,* for instance, mentions that the construction of a house should commence only on the days of fixed Nakshatras like Rohini, Uttara Phalguni, Uttara Ashada and Uttara Bhadrapada, as these will ensure a stable foundation for not just the physical home but for the household as well. [2] The *Brihat Samhita* lays down rules for placing the idols of Gods and declares the Nakshatras of Shravana, Pushya and Swati to be favourable for this because of their individual significations. [3] The idol of Lord Buddha, for instance, is particularly fruitful when placed on a Shravana day, perhaps because Lord Buddha is believed to an incarnation of Lord Vishnu with whom the asterism is connected. The text also mentions certain Nakshatras as facilitating deeds such as attempting harm to someone, summoning ghosts or separating two friends. Others will abet the destruction of property, arson and murder. [4] Yet others are auspicious if one wants to affect a sale, acquire knowledge, make a journey, or as the text *Nirnayasindhu* details, wear a new garment. [5]

In another text, *Muhurta Muktavali,* a thief may find his endeavours aided by auspicious timings—under the Nakshatras of Ashlesha, Mrigashira, Bharani, Swati, Dhanishta, Chitra and Anuradha, if they fall on a Saturday or a Tuesday and on earmarked dates. Some texts go so far as to declare that a newborn should be abandoned, for a few months or forever, if born under an inauspicious asterism. Kane expressed exhaustion at the firm hold of astrology on Indian minds and shared an example of how wrong it could go if one listened to astrologers blindly. His father's cousin, born under the Nakshatra of Mula, was considered unlucky at the time of his birth. The child's father was advised to abandon him at the foot of a sacred tree but he refused to do so. The father–son duo lived a long, happy life regardless of the predictions[6] and one shudders to imagine how it would have been, had the astrologers been heeded in this case.

The Hindu epic *Ramayana* offers another significant example of when the Nakshatras and Muhurtas didn't work as predicted. Even though Sage Vashistha had fixed what he thought was an auspicious time for the coronation of the heir of the Ikshavaku dynasty, Prince Rama, it brought on the eventful fourteen-year exile for him, his wife, Sita, and his brother, Lakshmana. An explanation suggested for this was the haste with which the Muhurta was fixed after King Dashratha dreamt about danger to his own life and his astrologers confirmed the threat. In order to appoint a king before his death, he asked the sage to find a Muhurta as soon as possible even if it met only the minimum criteria. The sage obliged; but right before the coronation, the King had to concede to Queen Kaikeyi's demand to send Lord Rama off to exile to fulfil a promise he had made to her years ago. It was her ploy to secure the throne for her own son Bharata. Dashratha, upon losing his eldest son, daughter-in-law and a younger son to a long exile soon died of grief. So, despite an auspicious Muhurta, destiny here did not care for the calculations of even the most renowned of sages and the wishes of the most influential of royals.

Stories of the Nakshatras

Coming to modern-day astrology, however, where do the Nakshatras fit in? If a kundli or birth chart is about the houses, signs and Grahas, then what do the asterisms represent? Where the former function more as main characters, acting out their roles on the centre stage, the asterisms work in the background because they show us what drives these characters. That is, Nakshatras point towards the patterns of the psychological make-up of an individual. As with the houses and signs, the Nakshatras too tell the story of the soul's journey through its earthly existence, but on an even deeper level. The first half of the word, Naksha, means to approach, whereas the second half, Tra, means to guard. Each Nakshatra is associated with a particular star, usually the brightest in its constellation. In the mythology of the Nakshatras, then, the brightest star(s) is a God or Goddess that helps guide the soul to its true purpose. Each of the nine Grahas is associated with three individual asterisms and we can peek into some stories of the Nakshatras connected to each to understand how this works.[7]

Venus' Bharani is the second of all Nakshatras and it lies in the constellation of Aries. It is the beginning of the Venusian energy amongst the Nakshatras. The soul enters its earthly body when the foetus develops in the human womb and so, this asterism is represented by the female reproductive organ. At the same time, however, its ruling deity is Yama, the God of death in the Hindu pantheon. Like Venus, then, Bharani is quite literally the representation of the cycle of life and death. This duality tells the story of those born under the influence of this asterism; their lives are all about creation but also turbulent and radical changes. Interestingly, the themes of life and death revolving around Bharani also reiterate the story of Quetzalcoatl and the association of Venus with Shukranu, or sperm, that we read before.

Krittika, the third Nakshatra, is ruled by the Sun. In addition to its story above, the Sun lends its bright light to this asterism and gives its natives penetrating insight, self-motivation and independence. These traits help the soul find its purification through knowledge and transformative experiences in life.

The fifth Nakshatra, Mrigashira, belongs to Mars. It is represented by four stars in the constellation of Orion. Its name translates to 'Deer's Head' and for an Indian reader it immediately calls forth the story from the Ramayana. The exiled royal couple of Ayodhya, Rama and Sita, accepted their fate gracefully and led a fairly uneventful life. That is, until a beautiful deer showed up. The subsequent chain of events that ensued resulted in the abduction of Sita and a battle between the armies of Rama and the demon king Ravana. On an individual level, the influence of the asterism can help one sense danger sooner than others. It also bestows other deer-like qualities such as gentleness and perpetual wandering or searching. In this Nakshatra, the soul's purpose is to wander through varied experiences in life before finding its true path.

Rahu's Ardra is the sixth. It too lies in the constellation of Orion and its energy lies in the star of Betelgeuse. It is ruled by Rudra, a fierce form of the God of destruction, Lord Shiva. The Hindu texts tell the tale of why Rudra came into existence. It so happened that Prajapati, the creator of the universe, began to lust after his daughter Usha, who was Dawn itself. To escape him, she took the form of a deer and escaped into a forest, but Prajapati became a deer as well, and pursued her. The Gods of the universe, collectively known as Vishvadevas, were horrified and outraged to witness this immorality. From their rage, Rudra was born and charged with the situation. He shot at Prajapati's deer form, decapitating him, which is where Mrigashira gets its origin story. The Gods, however, soon became remorseful at their part in this event. As a result, they abandoned Rudra who cried out in pain at being treated in such a manner. Rudra then became the hunter and the outcaste, living on the fringes of the society. This story outlines the themes of fighting what's wrong with the world, inner rage and a sense of abandonment that are peculiar to individuals who have Ardra in their birth chart. Like Rudra, these people tend to be the outsiders to their societal norms too. The asterism is represented as a teardrop, as Ardra individuals often suffer like Rudra did. Here the soul goes through intense internal storms in order to move forward in life.

Jupiter's Punarvasu is the seventh of all and is represented by the two bright stars of Gemini, Castor and Pollux. Its ruling deity is Aditi, the mother of all godly beings in the universe. She is the feminine principle— nurturing, receptive and in harmony. Karmically, it is the Nakshatra that helps the soul turn over a new leaf or begin again. It represents the first light after the storm that is Ardra. The symbology of this asterism is a quiver of arrows. The arrow that was shot by Ardra to achieve its goal is first met with confusion or rage before it induces change. Similarly, those born under this asterism often find success in their second attempts, not the first. This duality is expressed through its stars Castor, which creates losses, and Pollux, which brings back all that was lost. Rama too was a Punarvasu individual and his life story follows this arc as well; he had to earn back his kingdom after being banished to exile.

Ketu's Magha is the tenth and lies in the constellation of Leo. It is represented by the star of Regulus, one of the brightest stars in the night sky. Unlike other asterisms, it is more materialistically inclined as it is all about reaping the fruits of past lifetimes. Like its ruling Graha Ketu, Magha brings the past and present together, as individuals here inherit their wealth, whether it is expressed in the form of genes, material assets or knowledge, in order to build their current lives. It makes sense, then, that it is ruled by Pitris or the departed ancestors. The main objective of the soul here is to sustain the established order that one has inherited karmically and maintain control of that order.

Moon's Shravana is the twenty-second asterism. It is represented by three bright stars of the constellation Aquila, which lies near Capricorn. Its ruling deity is Lord Vishnu and it is from the story of his Vamana avatar that this Nakshatra draws its essence. The story starts with the king Bali, who had taken over the netherworld, earth, and heaven, many aeons ago. To deal with him, the gods turned to Lord Vishnu for help. He took the form of a young Brahmin boy, Vamana, and visited Bali when the latter was conducting a ritual, knowing that he could not refuse any request made of him by a Brahmin. So, when Bali asked what the young Vamana wanted, the request was for a land that could be covered with three strides of his feet. It seemed trivial to Bali and without heeding the warnings of one of his sages who had seen through this ruse by Lord Vishnu, the king granted the wish. At this, the young Brahmin started expanding into the form of Lord Vishnu, so large that with his first stride he covered the earth and the netherworld and with his second stride, he covered the heavens. For the third and last stride, he asked Bali where he should place his foot? The king, now humbled, bowed in response, and told him that the only thing he could offer now was his head. Astrologically, then, this Nakshatra is first and foremost about doing the right thing and being humble as Bali eventually learned. It is represented as an ear at times to highlight the importance of listening like Bali should have listened to the sage. Like Vishnu, it makes people born in Shravana tactful and shrewd in the achievement of their goals even though they often appear innocent and guileless. At this point, the soul's mission is to uphold the right order in the world through the qualities of this Nakshatra.

Saturn's Uttara Bhadrapada is the twenty-sixth asterism and is represented by two bright stars, one each from the constellations of Pegasus and Andromeda. It is the wise owl of all the Nakshatras and is associated with the symbols of both Vishnu, the one who maintains the world, and Shiva, the one who destroys. Its ruling deity Ahir Budhiyana is the serpent of the deep sea, which, like Vishnu, remains ever-elusive but maintains the order of the world on its head. But like Shiva, the serpent is not only a fierce warrior but also deals with dissolution on all levels of existence. Individuals born under this asterism, then, gain the wealth of the universe, be it spiritual or material, by destroying their illusions of life and the world. Just like the serpent that hides in the depth of the sea, their spirituality or wisdom is accessed in solitude.

Mercury's Revati is the last of the twenty-seven Nakshatras and lies in the constellation of Pisces. It is represented by the stars of Zeta-Piscium. This asterism has a lot to do with final enlightenment but does not necessarily signify Moksha, or the ultimate liberation from the cycle of birth and death. It is more concerned with the soul learning to see the bigger picture before it can embark upon a new cycle of life. This Nakshatra is the culmination of Mercurial energy as here the Graha literally has to become Buddha or the enlightened one. Its ruling deity, then, is Pushan, who lights up all paths; physical, mental, emotional and astral, in order to arrive at this final enlightenment.

Each of the twenty-seven Nakshatras is further divided into four parts, which gives a total of 108 divisions of the night sky. These parts are known as padas and have their own zodiacal rulers, which adds an even subtler flavour to the workings of that Nakshatra. So, where one might have a standard interpretation for a Pisces Moon sign, there will be a total of twelve possible interpretations as per Jyotish, as Pisces contains three Nakshatras and four padas for each of them. These Piscean Nakshatras are associated with different planets—Purva Bhadrapada with Jupiter, Uttara Bhadrapada with Saturn and finally, Revati with Mercury. Their Padas are further ruled by different Rasis or zodiac signs. So, the first part of Purva Bhadrapada is ruled by Aries, the second by Taurus, the third by Gemini and finally, the last by Cancer. The sequence is followed in Uttara Bhadrapada where its first part is ruled by Leo, second by Virgo, third by Libra and the fourth by Scorpio. So, the first part of Mercury's Revati is ruled by Sagittarius, the next by Capricorn, the third by Aquarius and the last one by Pisces.

This pattern is repeated in all of the twenty-seven Nakshatras, where the Grahas and Rasis add to a more nuanced interpretation in addition to the Nakshatra's story and the governing deity. Each of these placements yields a meaning that is unique on an emotional, mental and physical plane as well as the particular stage of development that the soul has to go through in the current lifetime.

More broadly, however, the psychological interpretations of Nakshatras help establish twenty-seven different archetypes in the modern Jyotish framework. For instance, where Magha is about honouring one's inherited tradition, Ardra is about breaking away from the norm after an internal turmoil and performing the role of the outsider. Where Bharani is about the cycle of life and death, Revati is about transcending the boundaries of emotion, thought and body. Where Krittika is about cutting through the illusions of society by means of knowledge and sharp mental faculties, Shravana is about the quieting down of the ego to receive spiritual guidance from providence. For a deeply traditional system of knowledge like Jyotish to accommodate such a wide range of human behaviours shows that these archetypes are not only timeless but universal as well, as they have always shown up in cultures across the world.

Stars in Other Astrological Systems

The stars, then, were not important only to the Hindu astrologers but other astrologers as well. The star Sirius, or the Dog Star, as we read before, was the harbinger of the renewal of life every year in ancient Egypt. It was also one of the fifteen Behenian Stars, mentioned in the German writer and thinker Henry Cornelius Agrippa's *Three Books of Occult Philosophy* (1530). These stars were a part of Arabic and European astrological systems, where the word Behenian comes from the Arabic word 'bahman' that means root. These included the Algol, Pleiades, Aldebaran, Capella, Regulus, Spica, Arcturus, Antares, Vega, Procyon, Alkaid, Algorab, Aphecca and Deneb Algedi. These stars are located in the zodiac constellations and were used to narrow down zodiacal astrological interpretations.

These stories may seem like stories from another world in our modern secular and rational world today. But nothing could be further from the truth. Astrological thought and stories have remained closely connected to our lives in more ways than we often realise. One of the ways in which astrology shows up in our lives is through our arts, literature, music and games. Through these, astrology hides in plain sight, and understanding this can open up a whole new perspective about how humans instinctively project their dramas onto the cosmos.

Notes

1   P.V. Kane, *History of Dharmashastra* (Bhandarkar Oriental Research Institute, 1962), p. 509.
2   Ibid., p. 622.
3   Ibid., p. 624.
4   Ibid., p. 559.
5   Ibid., p. 626.
6   Ibid., p. 633.
7   Prash Trivedi, *The Book of Nakshatras* (Sagar Publications, 2016), Komilla Sutton, *Essentials of Vedic Astrology* (Wessex Astrologer, 1999), Hart Defouw and Robert Svoboda, *Light on Life* (Penguin India, 2000).

8

Astrology in Our Lives:
In Arts, Literature and Music

The first known instance of astrology seeping into the artistic sphere is perhaps the earliest known depiction of the zodiac in the zodiac of Dendera This is an Egyptian bas-relief, originally a part of the Temple of Hathor, a temple complex in Dendera, Egypt. It is now on display at the Louvre Museum in Paris, having been transported there in the early nineteenth century. It depicts heaven as a disc, held up by four women with falcon-headed spirits as their assistants. Decans or the thirty-six spirits, figures from Egypt's native astrological concept, line the circumference to symbolise the 360 days of the Egyptian year. Along with the constellations, one can see Ursa Major and Draco as well. The planets are depicted in a certain sequence that occurs once every thousand years— Venus behind the constellation of Aquarius, Jupiter close to Cancer and Mars above Capricorn—which has led experts to narrow that particular skyscape down to a night between 15 June and 15 August 50 BCE. The relief also shows a lunar and solar eclipse that took place around that time.

A seventh or eighth century sculpture gave physical form to the Hindu astrological concept of Navagrahas, depicting the Sun, Moon and five planets as small figurines and Rahu as only a large head, and Ketu with the body of a snake. Another depiction of the Navagrahas can be found in a twelfth century Japanese painting, 'Descent of the Nine Luminaries and the Seven Stars at Kasuga'. It shows the luminaries as celestial beings, descending from the heavens into the Kasuga Shrine, a major religious site in Japan.

The celestial personification of the zodiac was a prominent artistic motif for Iranians as well. It was so prevalent that it permeated into works of art such as a twelfth century courtly bowl, a seventeenth century astronomical instrument and paintings showing the Sun and planets. In nearby Turkey, a thirteenth century Imperial Ottoman calendar commissioned by Sultan Abdulmecid I featured fourteen gouache panels showing the zodiac and other divine figures. These were decorated with gold and lacquer work, with traditional Persian floral motifs adding to their splendour.

A sword gifted to the French king, Henri IV, upon his marriage to Marie de Medici in December 1600 was decorated with the twelve zodiac signs, each of them accompanied by an inscription that listed out a warrior-like feat by the king. It was the golden age for astrology, especially in Europe, and the zodiac as an artistic motif was quite common at the time. It was also quite common to merge astronomy and astrology in an artistic fashion.

Andreas Cellarius' work as a Dutch–German cartographer brought together the cosmological ideas of medieval Europe's prominent astronomers and those of Ptolemy in his atlas, *Harmonica Macrocosmica*, published in 1660. It featured artistically decorated planispheres based on the astronomical models created by these men. Other works in the book include the zodiac as an elliptical belt around the Earth and as constellations in the northern and southern hemispheres, phases of Moon, and so on. A late seventeenth century engraving by the French artist Nicolas de Larmessian II, titled 'Costume of the Astrologer' showed an astrologer holding an armillary sphere and wearing a robe painted over with the constellations, stars, the Sun and the Moon. He was also shown holding books by Tycho Brahe and Copernicus in each of his arms, perhaps as a nod to the astronomical aspect of astrology.

Since love is what makes the world go round, the relationship of Mars and Venus as the quintessential male–female romantic liaison was another popular astrological motif used in art. It inspired a beautiful fifteenth-century painting by Renaissance painter Sandro Botticelli, known simply as 'Mars and Venus', as well as the 1824 painting titled 'Mars Being Disarmed by Venus' by the French painter Jacques Louis David.

English playwright William Shakespeare, on the other hand, helped immortalise the story of star-crossed lovers in his play Romeo and Juliet. The tragic and unfulfilled love story is one we have all heard at some point in our lives—Laila and Majnu, Tristan and Isolde, Heathcliff and Catherine Earnshaw, Heer and Ranjha are some other popular ones. The unfortunate couple in all of these stories are brought together by fate, fall in love and are then torn apart by fate of course, but often through death or madness. But in addition to this metaphorical use, Shakespeare also made over two hundred direct references to astrology in his plays, revealing a sound grasp of astrological principles rather than merely adopting them as literary props. His characters often mention planets, stars, eclipses, aspects, conjunctions and more,[1] to explain events around them or to foretell disaster. At times, he poked fun at the human tendency to ascribe personal failings to fate. For instance, in *Julius Caesar*, Cassius remarks, 'Men at some time are masters of their fates. The fault, dear Brutus, is not in our stars but in ourselves, that we are underlings,' implying that it was not fate that drove men to their decisions but their own innate tendencies. Similarly, in another popular play, *All's Well That Ends Well*, the character Helena says, 'Our remedies oft in ourselves do lie, which we ascribe to heaven: the fated sky. Gives us free scope, only doth backward pull; our slow designs when we ourselves are dull.'

Dante Alighieri was another literary giant who not only understood astrology but believed in it too. The Italian poet attributed his poetic gift to the constellation Gemini, the sign associated with communication and writing that dominated his chart. In his fourteenth century narrative poem, *Divine Comedy*, which is divided into three parts— *Inferno*, *Purgatorio* and *Paradiso*—we find a mention of not just planets, but astrologers as well. Inferno, which refers to the nine stages of Hell, features astrologers, fortune-tellers and soothsayers in the eighth circle of Hell for being frauds. Once one has passed through Hell and Purgatory, one reaches Heaven or Paradise. This Paradise is represented by celestial bodies, starting with the Moon, named the Inconstant. Next up is Mercury, the Ambitious. Then, Venus or the Lovers, followed by the Sun, the Wise; Mars, the Warriors of the Faith; Jupiter or the Just Rulers; and lastly Saturn, the Contemplatives. The eighth circle belongs to the Fixed Stars and finally, the ninth to the *Primum Mobile*, which is God itself. While he might not have liked astrologers, Dante did believe that events in our life and that of every living being on Earth were caused by the Heavens, which were more than just an anthropomorphic God. In another work, *Convivio*, he ascribed to the celestial luminaries the seven liberal arts—arithmetic to the Sun, grammar to the Moon, logic to Mercury, rhetoric to Venus, music to Mars, geometry to Jupiter and astronomy to Saturn.

The sixteenth century English poet Sir Philip Sidney wrote of his love for a woman who was betrothed to another man, in the 108 sonnets of *Astrophil and Stella*.

Astrophil here was Sidney himself, the star lover, and Stella was his love, the star. He wrote in Sonnet 26:

> Though earthbound wits dare to scorn astrology,
> And fools may think that those lamps of purest light
>   (the stars),
> Have birth-right in the sky for no purpose
> Except to spangle the black dress of night;
> Or for some dance, which in that high chamber,
> They should still go on treading to please a gazer's sight:
> As for me I know that Nature is not idle,
> And know that great causes result in great effects,
> And know that those higher bodies reign over lower ones.
> And if these laws were to fail, this proof satisfies me,
> That I often prophesy my future course,
> From just those two stars in Stella's face.

When the German writer Johann Wolfgang von Goethe wrote his biography, he saw it fit to begin it by writing down the coordinates of his place of birth on the first page. He followed that with, 'It was on the 28th of August 1749, at the stroke of twelve noon, that I came into the world at Frankfurt-on-Main. The constellation was auspicious: the Sun was in Virgo and at its culmination for the day. Jupiter and Venus looked amicably upon it, and Mercury was not hostile. Saturn and Mars maintained indifference. Only the Moon, just then becoming full, was in a position to exert adverse force, because its planetary hour had begun. It did, indeed, resist my birth, which did not take place until this hour had passed.'[2] While he never wrote about astrology anywhere else, this description betrays a good knowledge of the planets as well as his belief in astrology.

Saturn, the most feared planet across astrological systems, helped produce art and literature that was, well, Saturnian. Most intriguing are the paintings that show Saturn devouring his son, inspired by the Greek myth of Saturn doing so to thwart a prophecy that he would be defeated by his son. In Jacob Matham's 1597 series 'The Planets', Saturn is a young man who is seen biting into the belly of a baby. The most famous of these Saturn paintings was done by the Spanish Romantic painter Francisco Goya in the early nineteenth century and is known as one of his Black Paintings. He was likely inspired by the Dutch painter Peter Raul Ruben's Baroque depiction of the same idea two centuries ago. In both of these, Saturn is an old man holding a staff.

A feature common to all Saturn representations is that he is shown holding a staff or a sceptre in one hand, to mark his stature as the dispenser of justice or punishments.

However, the essence of Saturn was captured most lyrically by the noted American writer Henry Miller in his book *Colossus of Maroussi* (1941). He wrote, 'Saturn is a living symbol of gloom, morbidity, disaster, fatality ... Saturn is malefic through force of inertia ... Saturn is life in suspense, not dead so much as deathless, i.e. incapable of dying ... Saturn is postponement manifesting itself as an accomplishment in itself. Saturn is doubt, perplexity, scepticism, facts for facts' sake ... Saturn is the diabolical sweat of learning for its own sake, the congealed fog of the monomaniac's ceaseless pursuit of what is always just beyond his nose. Saturn is deliciously melancholic because it knows and recognises nothing beyond melancholy; it swims in its own fat ... Saturn is as eternal as fear and irresolution, growing more milky, more cloudy with each compromise, each capitulation ... Saturn gives us only what we ask for, never an ounce extra.'

In 1995, the German writer W.G. Sebald wrote about his pilgrimage through the English town of Suffolk in his semi-autobiographical novel, *The Rings of Saturn*. The work spans various arcs of history, including the Holocaust. He never specifically explains the title, but one can perhaps intuit that he understood the mythology of Saturn when, in a chapter, he wrote, 'The shadow of the night is drawn like a black veil across the Earth, and since almost all creatures, from one meridian to the next, lie down after the Sun has set, so, he continues, one might, in following the setting Sun, see on our globe nothing but prone bodies, row upon row, as if levelled by the scythe of Saturn—an endless graveyard for a humanity struck by falling sickness.'

The author's deep dive into his life feels like navel-gazing, and at one point, he references the noted English polymath, doctor and writer, Sir Thomas Browne, a self-confessed melancholic. Sebald wrote, 'There is no antidote [Browne writes], against the opium of time. The winter Sun shows how soon the light fades from the ash, how soon night enfolds us. Hour upon hour is added to the sum. Time itself grows old. Pyramids, arches and obelisks are melting pillars of snow. Not even those who have found a place amidst the heavenly constellations have perpetuated their names: Nimrod is lost in Orion, and Osiris in the Dog Star. Indeed, old families last not three oaks.' This lament of decay, melancholia and the general heaviness of the book once again point to Saturn, even though this was not intentional on Sebald's part.

But there was a wordsmith who was quite intentional about his astrology—Nobel Prize winner and celebrated Irish poet William Butler Yeats. He was an expert astrologer, and astrological themes centring on the Moon, fate and destiny often showed up in his work. His first influence might have been his uncle, George Pollexfen, the man who first drew up his birth chart. He predicted Yeats' literary brilliance, an intense love affair with Maud Gonne and hinted at the many other women who were to become a part of his life. Yeats took an active interest in astrology and tarot cards right from his twenties; he would later focus mostly on the former. In her diary, English novelist Virginia Woolf mentions a conversation with Yeats, writing, 'He believes entirely in horoscopes. Will never do business with anyone without having their horoscopes.' This was in November 1930, around the same time he wrote the following in an unpublished work, titled *Seven Propositions*—'Human life is either the struggle of a destiny against all other destinies or a transformation of the character defined in the horoscope into timeless and spaceless existence. The whole passage from birth to birth should be an epitome of the whole passage of the universe through time, and back into its timeless and spaceless condition.'

Apart from literature and art, astrological thought found resonance in music as well. The English composer Gustav Holst wrote a seven-piece orchestral suite called

'The Planets' between 1914 and 1916. While his music was unmistakably Victorian, it also had prominent Sanskrit themes with some of his previous compositions named as Indra (1903), Sita (1906) and Savitri (1908-09). It is believed that The Planets was similarly inspired. It was played in part in September 1918 at London's Queen's Hall, but the first complete performance only took place two years later at the London Symphony Orchestra. Holst, who called astrology his 'pet vice', explained his work thus, 'These pieces were suggested by the astrological significances of the planets. There is no programme music in them, neither have they any connection with the deities of classical mythology bearing the same names. If any guide to the music is required, the subtitle to each piece will be found sufficient ... For instance, Jupiter brings jollity in the ordinary sense, and also the more ceremonial type of rejoicing associated with religions or national festivities. Saturn brings not only physical decay, but also a vision of fulfilment. Mercury is the symbol of the mind.'[3]

The first part of the suite belongs to the fiery red planet and is titled 'Mars, The Bringer of War'. Perhaps it made sense to start with it, given that the suite was written in the aftermath of the First World War. The piece opens with vigour and the music maintains a high tempo throughout, as one would expect from a work with such a title. Composer John Williams was so inspired by Mars that he even modelled the Star Wars' Imperial March theme after it.[4]

After Mars comes a markedly more pleasing 'Venus, the Bringer of Peace'. Next up is the shortest section of the suite, titled 'Mercury, the Winged Messenger', which uses the celesta, a non-traditional piano where the hammers strike metallic bars instead of strings. After this is 'Jupiter, the Bringer of Jollity', the most famous of all the sections. It has a radiance and joy to it and has often been incorporated into other works. This includes the popular English hymn, 'I Vow to Thee, My Country', which was played at the funerals of Sir Winston Churchill, Princess Diana and former prime minister Margaret Thatcher, besides being performed at Britain's annual Remembrance Day celebrations.

Following Jupiter in the suite is 'Saturn, the Bringer of Old Age'. Holst's personal favourite from his work, Saturn is a slow rhythmic melody performed on flutes and harps. Concluding the suite, we have 'Uranus, the Magician', and 'Neptune, the Mystic', where the former is rather eccentric and the latter is a delicate work which is supposed to lack almost any distinctive character. The entire suite is almost fifty minutes long.

Almost a century before Holst, Muthuswami Dikshitar, one of the musical trinity of Indian Carnatic music, had composed his own series of songs that brought together music and astrology. Born in 1775 in Tamil Nadu, Dikshitar began his career as a composer in 1799. The seven Navagraha Kritis[5] composed by him are amongst his best-known work. Legend has it that when his student Tambiappa Pillai[6] fell ill, Dikshitar, who possessed a working knowledge of Jyotish, checked his horoscope. He found that a malefic influence of Jupiter was causing Pillai a stomach ailment. To remedy this, Dikshitar wrote 'Brhaspate' in praise of Jupiter and taught it to Pillai. Pillai was soon cured of his ailment after singing this song for some time every day. Seeing this, Dikshitar was inspired to compose songs for the other planets as well. These compositions are 'Suryamurta' for the Sun; 'Chandram Bhaja' for the Moon; 'Angarakam Ashrayami' for Mars; 'Budham Ashrayami' for Mercury; 'Sri Sukra Bhagavantam' for Venus and 'Divakaradanujam' for Saturn. Written in Sanskrit, each of these pieces has a distinctive raga (melodic framework) and tala (rhythmic beat). They are collectively known as the 'Vaara Kritis', i.e., everyday Kritis that are meant to be sung on the day of that Graha.[7] There are two more, for Rahu and Ketu, which were written by Dikshitar's students but credited to him. It takes little over an hour to perform all the Vaara Kritis. Unlike Holst's work, these songs are a part of everyday life in India, especially in South India, and for lovers of Carnatic music, having been sung and heard continuously since the early twentieth century.

These Kritis are songs of praises for the Grahas and are filled with mythological stories from the Hindu canon as well as astrological principles. More specifically, they tap into the Jyotish notion that a Graha's malefic influence can be remedied or a benefic influence can be further accentuated by praying to that Graha on a day that is rich with its vibrations. So, if one wants the good graces of the Sun bestowed upon them, the ideal day to sing or listen to Suryamurta would be Sunday, with the song starting off with, 'Oh illuminator of all infinite causes and effects in the world, the Lord of Simha (Leo) Rasi/One whose effulgent lustre has been praised by those of highest esteem, the bestower of benefits such as good health.' The Sun is also referred to as the one whose chariot is driven by seven divine horses, which can represent several meanings, such as the seven days of the week, seven sacred meters of verse or the seven colours of light.

Chandra's song belongs to Mondays. Dikshitar refers to the Moon as the mind in his first verse, which is in line with how Hindu astrology perceives the luminary's significance to human life. The song further refers to the Moon as the follower and attendant of Madana, the infatuator, Manmatha, the God of love and Kama, the God of desire. The Moon is also described as the Lord of the stars, or Nakshatras, and by the markings on its surface that resemble a hare, i.e., the Moon rabbit, or Shashank, discussed previously.

Next comes the 'Angaraka', or the song of Mars, which belongs to Tuesday, or Mangalvar, since Mars is known as Mangal in Hindi. The red planet's attributes are highlighted as, '[he] who is the Lord of the cherished houses of Mesa (Aries) and Vrischika (Scorpio), with red limbs, who wears the red dress and is the bearer of the sword and trident/The auspicious one, with beautiful neck, with lovely feet, bestower of auspiciousness, riding on the Goat, and whose higher aphelion is in Makara (Capricorn) Rasi.' The song also mentions the Vaidisvaran Temple in Thanjavur as the place to visit to remedy an afflicted Mars.

After this is the song of Budha, or Mercury. It highlights Mercury's universal connection with intelligence by describing it as holding a book in hand and as the 'bestower of the sweet art of poetry, the one of splendorous wealth'. In tune with Hindu astrological principles, Mercury is anointed Lord of the houses of Mithuna (Gemini) and

Kanya (Virgo). Jupiter, or Brihaspati, on the other hand, lords over the houses of Dhanu (Sagittarius) and Meena (Pisces) and is referred to as the Lord of the universe as well as the manifester of the four phases of speech, among other descriptors.

Dikshitar refers to Venus, or Shukra, as 'Shri Shukra Bhagavantam' or as God Shukra. As a musician, it was only apt for Dikshitar to worship the planet of art and music. The song mentions that Venus is the Lord of Tula (Libra) and Vrishabh (Taurus) and also describes it as an enemy of the Sun and Jupiter. It also touches upon a host of other astrological principles, such as base-triplicity of the planets, different kinds of birth charts as per Jyotish and the degrees in these charts.

Finally, there is the song of Shani, or Saturn, to be meditated upon on a Saturday. This planet is referred to as the slow-moving and the courageous one 'who causes fear in people plunged in the ocean of worldly existence and is the harbinger of calamitous events'—a portrayal akin to how Saturn is described across different astrological systems. The planet is also always depicted as an old man carrying a staff, and so Dikshitar sings, 'whose knee was disfigured by the staff of the Lord of the Death'. The planet, which rules the houses of Makara (Capricorn) and Kumbha (Aquarius), is called 'the fire capable of splitting the time wheel', alluding to its nature of causing delays and obstructions in a person's life.

Astrology, then, was never on the sidelines of society. It was, in fact, deeply ingrained in various aspects of life and quite often, without even realising it, we have heard and told its stories even in the modern world. We have often spoken of fate and destiny without understanding that it is that very instinct that has kept astrology alive across the world for thousands of years. While claims of being able to divine the future or the mystical have always been controversial, there have been many figures throughout history who dabbled in it. Some did it out of curiosity and others, for personal gain. In doing so, they brought astrology to the forefront in ways that were unexpected, but made it all the more relevant.

Notes

1   Bobrick Benson, *Fated Sky: Astrology in History* (Simon and Schuster, 2006), p. 180.
2   Ibid., p. 255.
3   Program Notes, 'Holst: The Planets' (San Francisco Symphony, 2018), https://www.sfsymphony.org/Data/Event-Data/Program-Notes/H/Holst-The-Planets.
4   Tom Huizenga, 'The Planets at 100' (NPR, 2018), https://www.npr.org/sections/deceptivecadence/2018/09/28/652700640/the-planets-at-100-a-listener-s-guide-to-holst-s-solar-system.
5   Todd M. McComb, *Navagraha Kritis of Muthuswamy Dikshithar* (Medieval.org, year unknown), http://www.medieval.org/music/world/carnatic/lyrics/navagraha.html.
6   Sriram V., *Dikshithar's Navagraha Kritis* (Madras Heritage and Carnatic Music, 2011), https://sriramv.wordpress.com/2011/02/24/dikshitars-navagraha-kritis/.
7   Lakshmi Venkatraman, 'Seven Kritis for Seven Days' (*The Hindu*, 2010), https://www.thehindu.com/features/friday-review/history-and-culture/Seven-kritis-for-seven-days/article15576597.ece.

9

Influential Thinkers on Astrology:
Eureka or Bah! Humbug

Astrology, as polarising as it has always been, has been difficult to ignore even for great thinkers and leaders. It was through their own explorations of astrology that these thinkers ended up legitimising it for society at large, for better or for worse. Understanding the appeal of astrology from their unique perspectives is important to understand how astrology has taken shape since the advent of civilisation.

In *Manusmriti,* an ancient Sanskrit text, those who earn their living through astrology are listed among priests who should not be invited to religious rites, including those for departed ancestors. The text prohibits ascetics from making predictions from studying omens in nature, palms or lunar asterisms in order to secure food or money for themselves. However, the reason behind this is atypical—it's not out of disdain for astrology but the belief that such activities create Karma that can pollute an individual.[1]

In Rome, Cicero, the philosopher and statesman, questioned astrology by posing the question as to how twins could have different destinies although born under the same constellation. Satirist and poet Juvenal mocked the high-society women of his time for constantly checking their birth charts for auspiciousness of undertaking an activity, even for applying ointments to a sore.[2] However, philosophers Seneca and Marcus Aurelius, considered to be the giants of the school of stoicism, believed in a larger scheme of things that aligned with astrological thought. Seneca, who was also a dramatist, believed that whatever happened was a sign of something that was to come next. Aurelius, on the other hand, encouraged his readers to accept everything that happened, however disagreeable, because it led to the 'health of the universe'.

Kautilya, the master Indian administrator, philosopher and economist, found extreme reliance on astrology reprehensible. However, he acknowledged that a king should appoint a Purohit, or priest, who was well-versed in all six Angas of the Vedas, including Vedanga Jyotish. This astrologer must belong to a respectable family and have an unimpeachable character. If these conditions were met, the king must follow the priest like a student follows his teacher. His Italian counterpart, Niccolo Machiavelli, did not understand how astrology worked, but accepted it as valid because he had observed that astrologers would always predict the occurrence of major events well before they came to pass.[3]

Brahe and Kepler

While we distinguish between an astrologer and an astronomer today, this wasn't the case well until the seventeenth century. Tycho Brahe, the Danish astronomer, was only twenty-eight years old when he was declared a national treasure by King Frederick II of Denmark in 1574. A couple of years before this proclamation, he had been the first to ever spot a nova, or a new star, in the constellation of Cassiopeia, writing of it, 'It surpassed all the other stars in its brilliance and was shining directly above my head; and since I had, from boyhood, known all the stars of the heavens perfectly, it was quite evident to me that there had never been any star in that place of the sky, even the smallest, to say nothing of a star so conspicuous and bright as this.' This nova was then visible to the naked eye for more than a year after this, changing its colour from bright white to a faint red before disappearing into nothingness forever. Brahe, a Protestant, thought that it perhaps foretold the end of the Roman Catholic Church, an early indication of his astrological beliefs.

Apart from this, Brahe also worked on tracking the movements of the planets after he found that existing planetary tables were insufficient. All this work not only earned him his reputation but also an estate on a Swedish island. There he set up Uraniborg, named after Urania, the muse of astronomy and the great granddaughter of the Greek God Uranus. Uraniborg was an underground observatory where Brahe and his assistants 'remapped the visible sky'. This team had access to the finest astronomical instruments available in Europe, even though the telescope hadn't been invented yet. Interestingly, the day of its launch was chosen astrologically, i.e., 8 August 1576 was selected because the Sun and Jupiter were rising and this promised fame to the venture.[4]

As an astronomer–astrologer, Brahe considered eclipses to be generally bad for kings and princes as, according to him, the Sun and the Moon were princes among the planets; and cited examples of royals that had passed away following an eclipse to support his theory. Most importantly, he served as the court astrologer to the Danish king. When the king's son Christian IV was born, Brahe made several predictions about his personality, life events and eventual death. He said that the prince was at risk at the ages of twelve, twenty-nine and fifty-six, but if he survived all these events, he would live up to a ripe old age. The prince lost his father at the age of eleven and did live till the age of seventy-one, so it could be said that Brahe's predictions were not completely off the mark. However, it was also under Christian IV's reign that he was ousted from the kingdom because of his difficult personality and an overly luxurious lifestyle that began to drain the king's coffers.

After this unceremonious ouster, Brahe moved to

Bohemia and became the imperial mathematician to Emperor Rudolph II. He was soon joined by Johannes Kepler as his assistant in 1600. The two worked together for a year and a half, most notably on their ephemerides, the Rudolphine Tables named after their king. The work mapped out stellar and planetary movements the most precisely they had ever been until then and proved useful to both astronomers and astrologers for decades to come. But in October 1601, Brahe passed away and Kepler had to work all on his own. He moved on to other projects and only managed to complete the Tables in 1623, which took another four years to be printed for public use.

The student, however, proved to be more impressive than the mentor. Kepler's work as an astronomer was groundbreaking, and he was also a more ardent astrologer than Brahe. But unlike Brahe, he had quite a rough start in life. He grew up poor and his family life veered wildly from one misadventure to other. At one point, he drew up astrological sketches describing his father as vicious because of the placement of Mars in his birth chart and poor because of Jupiter. Kepler considered himself reckless as well, which he thought was inevitable 'due to Mars in square to Mercury trine Moon' in his own chart. Before he started working with Brahe, Kepler had also published an astrological almanac. He had made two major predictions in the almanac, one about an invasion and the other about climate, both of which came true and earned him some recognition. He went on to publish eighteen more almanacs in his lifetime.[5]

Kepler's view of the cosmos was decidedly mystical.

He saw a divine order and a musical arrangement to the universe, which guided his work on planetary motion. In his conception, the Sun corresponded to the C note, Saturn to D, Mercury to E, Moon to F, Mars to G, Venus to A and Jupiter to B. In terms of vocals, Saturn and Jupiter were bass, Mars the tenor, Venus the contralto and Mercury the soprano.

Amongst his astrological beliefs was a great conjunction theory about historical epochs. So, a Mars–Saturn conjunction, in his view, foretold civil strife. Venus conjunct Mars brought climatic turbulence but a Jupiter and Mars one brought clear skies.

Kepler wrote about books about astrology to bust astrological myths and introduce ideas developed by him. One of his ideas was that of 'astral heredity', according to which there was a connection between parents' charts and their children, particularly the firstborn. In his book, *The Third Man Intervening or Tertius Interveniens* (1610), he wrote about how when a baby took birth, a picture of sorts of the sky was imprinted upon the soul that would then go on to dictate the individual's temperament and life. His other two books on the topic were *On the Fundamentals of Astrology and Report on the Fiery Triplicity*.

Throughout his life, Kepler cast many horoscopes, at least eight hundred of which still exist today. Notable among these was that of Count Albrecht von Wallenstein, best known as a military leader who fought on the German side during the Thirty Years' War (1618–1648). But the chart reading, sought ten years before this war, was a blind one. Kepler did not know who he was reading for. But it was accurate enough for Wallenstein to seek another reading from him in 1624. In this reading, Kepler could see the decorated war general's death in ten years but demurred from mentioning it.[6] Wallenstein passed away in 1634.

In fact, Kepler was so adept at astrology that when his own time came, he knew about that as well. In November 1630, when Kepler set out for some work in Poland, he seemed to have known that he would die on the way, for he put his affairs and finances in order before he left. At the age of fifty-eight, he suddenly collapsed for no apparent reason mid-journey in Regensburg, Germany. His tombstone marks him as the 'prince of astronomy' and his self-composed epitaph reads, 'My soul being from heaven, I measured the star-filled skies;/Now I measure a hollow plot of earth where a shadow of me lies.'

While many tend to separate Kepler from his astrology in historical accounts of his science, he was undoubtedly a staunch believer and practitioner. He also railed against those who misused or ridiculed astrology but believed that once the mud and dirt was sorted away, a sound and useful body of knowledge would emerge as a result.

Vivekananda and Ramanujan

Swami Vivekananda, one of Hinduism's most revered thinkers known for introducing Advaita Vedanta and yoga to the West, strongly eschewed astrology. Born in 1863 in Kolkata, Vivekananda was instrumental in reforming Hinduism and rescuing it from ignorance and superstition. While he acknowledged astrologers who predicted well, he believed it was more a reading of the mind than of the stars. In some cases, it was even 'arrant trash'.[7] He had more faith in the power of self-belief and self-knowledge to traverse the vagaries of life because the 'excessive attention to the minutiae of astrology is one of the superstitions which has hurt the Hindus very much'. To him, a belief in astrology and mystical influences was the sign of a weak mind, and he advised people to see a good physician and take rest when struck by such thoughts.

But an influential contemporary of his, the celebrated mathematician Srinivasa Ramanujan, was a strong believer in astrology and very much into the occult. Born in 1887 in Tamil Nadu, Ramanujan carved an international and enduring legacy for himself as a mathematician despite little formal training in the subject. He was not only interested in astrology but had a penchant for interpreting dreams and reading palms as well. But while it was all par for the course in India, his friends and colleagues at Cambridge were often hard-pressed to accept this side of him. Robert Kanigel in his Ramanujan biography *The Man Who Knew Infinity*[8] noted that the mathematician's belief in hidden and unseen forces was never an issue as long as he was in India. In fact, he often felt free to act on his 'irrational' impulses, even where mathematics was concerned, much to the chagrin of his colleagues.

Ramanujan is believed to have found his calling for mathematics through a dream, prepared astrological projections for people and fixed auspicious times for religious functions for relatives and friends. By studying his own palm, he predicted his own death before the age of thirty-five and even told his friends about it. He did die very young in 1920, aged only thirty-two.

His worldview, not unlike Kepler, was a blend of mystical imagination and raw intellect. Because he grew up in India, he was greatly influenced by Hindu philosophy and its many deities. Once, while travelling in an electric streetcar, he remarked to a friend, 'That man imagines he has the power to go slow or fast at his pleasure. He forgets that he gets the power through the current that flows in the overhead wires ... That is the way maya (illusion in English) works in this world.' As Jyotish is intimately connected to Hinduism, it's not hard to see why he found it natural to dabble in astrology.

But, much like Kepler, many seek to separate the man from his beliefs, including G.H. Hardy, the man who was instrumental in arranging Ramanujan's stint at Cambridge. While he is renowned for his extraordinary mathematical genius, many who come from empirical intellectual traditions are still decidedly uncomfortable with his unconventional methods and want to explain them away as an unfortunate eccentricity.

Astrology in Politics

A few decades later, astrologers played an important role in the Second World War. A fake German astrology magazine, *Der Zenit*, was published by an astrologer in British employ for propaganda purposes in 1942–43.

The magazine ran for a total of six issues and would publish exact descriptions of events that had happened as predictions by pre-dating the issue. The accuracy, then, seemed eerie. *Der Zenit* soon caught the attention of the German high command. Once the British made sure of that, misleading information was published as predictions to deter Germans from various military and patrolling activities in March 1943.[9] Hitler, while personally wary and loathsome of astrologers for their unsavoury predictions about his life and career, did hire astrologers for the party's propaganda work.

Fast forward a few more decades and we come to Ronald Reagan, one of the most influential American presidents ever. The first indication of Reagan's inclination towards astrology came to light when he chose to take oath as the governor of California at 12.10 a.m. on 2 January 1967. He was also friends with the astrologer Carroll Righter, as mentioned in his biography, *Where's the Rest of Me?*, and likely consulted with him during the 60s and the 70s.

After him, it was Joan Quigley who became the Reagan couple's go-to astrologer until the 80s. But this proved to be a much more contentious association after details of it emerged in a book by the president's chief of staff, Donald Regan, in 1988. The book, *For the Record: From Wall Street to Washington,* claimed that a large part of the president's schedule was managed astrologically based on advice from Quigley. This was confirmed by a White House statement which did not deny the claim but instead asserted that it had no effect on policy decisions. However, the book claimed that even key decisions such as the invasion of Grenada, the attack on Libya and negotiations with Mikhail Gorbachev were cleared with astrologers first. Even the signing of the Intermediate-Range Nuclear Forces Treaty with Russia in 1987 was signed on a day and time that was astrologically advised, according to the book.[10]

The official version was that Nancy Reagan had become particularly invested in astrology after the assassination attempt on her husband in 1981 and that it was more of an emotional crutch than a sincere belief. However, the damage was done, and the Reagans' use of astrology became the butt of jokes. A report in *The New York Times* from May 1988 mentions some of them—'On Capitol Hill, Representative Tony Coelho, the Democratic whip, expressed amazement at Republican objections to a revised trade bill and said, "Maybe an astrologer is telling them to object today" to which Speaker of the House, Jim Wright, says, "It's all right with me. I'm glad he consults somebody."' The same report mentions President Theodore Roosevelt and Franklin D. Roosevelt as being inclined towards astrology and horoscopes too. However, this fracas became so bitter that Quigley ended up writing about her experiences advising the Reagans in her book, *What Does Joan Say,* to set the record straight.

Around the same time as Reagan's reign, the Indian prime minister, Indira Gandhi, would exhibit an unhealthy reliance on astrologers too. M.O. Mathai, the private secretary to her father, the first prime minister of India Jawaharlal Nehru, narrates an incident about Gandhi's earlier trysts with astrology in his book, *My*

Days With Nehru.[11] On one particular evening, the PM and his secretary drove to a cabinet minister's house where Nehru told Mathai to go back home and send the car back for him in some time. But when he reached the prime minister's house, Gandhi was upset that he had left her father alone as his horoscope indicated 'that one of his legs will be disabled'. She thought he might meet with a car accident and should be accompanied by someone at all times. At her behest, he drove back to the minister's place and explained to Nehru his reasons for showing up. Nehru, wrote Mathai, said, 'Why did you listen to her bilge? You should have laughed it away.'

In 1963, just before the start of her influential political career, Gandhi met a Tamil Christian astrologer–palmist whose name Mathai never mentions. He does, however, say that the person who used to put Gandhi and the astrologer in touch was Maragatham Chandrashekar, the first special envoy of the prime minister. The astrologer's prediction about the assassination of the then Prime Minister of Ceylon, now Sri Lanka, had come true. So, when he said that Gandhi was going to become the prime minister within three years and would stay at the helm till 1977, he was taken seriously. This prediction proved to be correct as well and he became a regular at Gandhi's office before he was shunted out by her staff. After him, Dhirendra Brahmachari, the controversial yoga guru and astrologer, became her resident counsellor. Of his iron-clad hold over her, it was said, 'He sees the prime minister almost every day. He orders her servants around. He frightens her officials, who toady to him because he is so close to the nation's leader, and they fear a transfer to somewhere remote and nasty if they offend him in any way.' Brahmachari was described as a fraud by many, including Mathai.

But while it might have made sense for astronomers, mathematicians and world leaders to delve deeply into astrology, even having astrologers at their beck and call, the general populace in the world was generally at the mercy of a neighbourhood priest or had to travel far and wide in order to seek astrological counsel. Even then, the best one could get was a brief prognostication. Most people did not know how astrology worked, what a birth chart looked like or what their own astrological placements meant. That began to change in the twentieth century as astrology went through major shifts in a sequence of events which, while unrelated to each other, helped advance the story of astrology.

Notes

1   P.V. Kane, *History of Dharmashastra* (Bhandarkar Oriental Research Institute, 1962), p. 527.
2   Bobrick Benson, *Fated Sky: Astrology in History* (Simon and Schuster, 2006), p. 32.
3   Ibid., p. 123.
4   Ibid., p. 153.
5   Ibid., p. 162.
6   Ibid., pp. 170-171.
7   Swami Vivekananda, *Swami Vivekananda on Astrology* (Sreyas Foundation, 2010), https://english.sreyas.in/swami-vivekananda-on-astrology/.

8 Robert Kanigel, *The Man Who Knew Infinity* (Abacus, 1992), p. 282.

9 Bobrick Benson, *Fated Sky: Astrology in History* (Simon and Schuster, 2006), p. 287.

10 Chris Brennan, 'Joan Quigley and the Reagans' Use of Astrology' (The Astrology Podcast, 2016), https://theastrologypodcast.com/2016/03/08/joan-quigley-reagan-and-astrology/.

11 M.O. Mathai, *My Days With Nehru* (Vikas Publishing House, 1980), pp. 20-22.

10

Birth of Horoscopes:
What's Your Sun Sign

Unless one is really into astrology, what most people today understand as astrology is really just their Sun sign placement according to tropical astrology. How did we get here, considering the extraordinary labour of the many, many stargazers and thinkers before us? It might have something to do with the disentanglement of astrology and astronomy post the Copernican revolution.

While astrology never completely dropped off from the face of Earth, it was decidedly out of favour with both science and religion by the early eighteenth century in Europe. As we have noted before, Western society was

undergoing two radical changes at this time. In addition
to the shift of the model of the universe from a geocentric
to a heliocentric one, the rise of the Roman Catholic
Church had a part to play as well. Astrology threatened
the Vatican's authority to shape public discourse on God
and the cosmos and so, it came to be regarded as not
only technically unsound but also immoral. It didn't help
that the astrologers of the time had begun to venture
out of their remit and would make increasingly bold and
politically dangerous predictions. All in all, irrespective
of Brahe and Kepler's explorations of astrology, most of
intellectual and polite society decided that it had to go.
So astrologers went underground. That is, for a century or
so. Towards the end of the nineteenth century, astrology
began to see a momentous revival. The stage for this was
set up by four astrologers in particular, whose work would
go on to change the very face of astrology.

The first of these was William Frederick Allan, who can
be termed as the only salesman astrology has ever had.[1]
Born in 1860 in the United Kingdom, his upbringing
was marked by his mother's devout Anglican beliefs and
a father who left the family when Allan was nine years
old. In his mid-twenties, he was managing a grocery store
in Manchester when he fell ill. But instead of going to a
regular doctor, he visited a Dr Richardson who was both
an herbalist and an astrologer. The doctor not only cured
him of his kidney ailment but also set him on his life
path by introducing him to astrology. After that, Allan
studied astrology as an enthusiast for years and even wrote
articles for the magazine of an occult society, *Celestial
Brotherhood*, of which he was a member. His newfound

beliefs were reflected in his identity when he changed his name to Alan Leo, as he is better known today, to correspond to his own astrological Sun sign.

He subscribed to many astrology-related journals and through one of those, *The Astrologer*, he met his future business partner Frederick Lacey who would further lead Leo to the biggest influence of his astrological journey, the Theosophists. Soon enough, he started spending a lot of time at the headquarters of the Theosophical Society in London while still working as a travelling salesman.

Theosophy and Astrology

The story of theosophy is vital to the revival of astrology as we know it today. Established by the Ukraine-born Helena Blavatsky as a society in New York City in 1875, it brought the ideas of Karma and Reincarnation into a Western mould of spirituality. Before she set up the society, Blavatsky had spent two decades travelling around the world, including India where she stayed for two years. But while her stay wasn't all that remarkable, she would later meet a Hindu man named Morya in London in 1851. She claimed that she had had visions of him as a child and so when he instructed her to visit Tibet, she attempted to travel there, and there are reports that claim she did manage to make it out there even though it was virtually impossible for a woman to do so. In any case, by the end of her travels, she had developed theosophy as a religion. It was a synthesis of Indian, Platonic, Hermetic and Kabbalistic thought.

According to her, there was an absolute first cause in the universe and the potential of that first cause made human life possible. The goal of life, then, was to realise that potential over a period of many lifetimes and unite the soul with the absolute. While this is in line with the Hindu view of the soul's ultimate aim of Moksha or liberation from the cycle of life and death, there is an offshoot to this that was proposed by Christianity-oriented theosophists. For them, the realisation of potential or the awakening is really 'Christ consciousness' which would be felt by everyone living through the Age of Aquarius, which pointed to revolutions in the areas of government, technology and industry[2] in the twentieth century. But whatever view one subscribed to, the final aim was to achieve the unity of the individual soul with the absolute until the entire cosmos dissolved into the Pure Spirit. For this, every individual must do whatever it took to awaken their spiritual awareness, including astrology, yoga and aromatherapy, among other practices.[3] At its peak, the society had 45,000 members, with more than hundred lodges in the Indian subcontinent. In 1882, the society's international headquarters shifted from New York City to Adyar in Madras (now Chennai).

Theosophy gained relevance in the Western world because it emerged at a time when religion was becoming private and a lack of spiritual communion was felt in the public arena. Leo was highly impressed with theosophical thought and would go on to form his own ideas about how astrology could help with the core mission as outlined by the religion. He became privy to Blavatsky's inner circle through her astrologer and became a member of the society in 1890. In August that year, his business partner Lacey and he decided to launch a publication, *The Astrologer's Magazine*.

The magazine featured articles on astrology but it was the offer to readers to send in their birth details for a free reading that really changed it all. People were soon writing to them with their time, date and place of birth; for short, personalised horoscopes. In the next four years, the two sent out about four thousand such readings. While Lacey had to bow out of the venture, owing to other work commitments, another significant person entered Leo's life at this time. This person was Ada Burch, often called Bessie, also a theosophist. She had written in to ask for a reading and had found the final product to be impressive enough. The pair met in person in early 1893 and discovered that they enjoyed each other's company. Burch was married at the time but her husband had been unable to keep up with her condition of a platonic relationship and the couple had separated. Leo, on the other hand, was happy to oblige. They married soon after and as practising theosophists, the couple gave up meat, alcohol and smoking. His marriage made his religious convictions even stronger and it reflected in his now renamed magazine, *Modern Astrologer*, which often carried articles written from a theosophical perspective. The theosophists too started publishing Leo's articles and helped spread his astrological ideas through their lodges across the world.

In 1903, one of his employees suggested to Leo a way

to organise his material in order to streamline the free readings. Doing that proved to be more than just efficient. Leo essentially assembled a production line for all possible placements of the Sun, Moon and the planets in different signs and most of his written material was plagiarised from various astrological books. Kim Farnell, Leo's biographer, quotes from the works of Edward Harold Bailey who was his staff member and was opposed to Leo's approach towards astrology, 'The whole of the mimeographed sheets comprising his test horoscopes were copies, in many cases verbatim, from Sepharial's *Prognostications from the Rising Sign* and H.S. Green's *Planets in Signs and Houses*, while the greater part of the other sheets of his system were copied and paraphrased from Butler's *Solar Biology*.'[4]

But he had no compunctions about this and filled up his office with hundreds of sheets of such written material. This was a newer and improved form of reading and so this was advertised as a 'test horoscope' or 'shilling horoscope', since these horoscopes were priced at a shilling. The idea worked because in the next three years, Leo did over twenty thousand such readings. For twenty-five pounds, readers could get an even more detailed analysis. An unintended and far-reaching consequence of this was that many copied this idea, and soon enough, there were scores of opportunists giving out these readings to make a quick buck. Astrology was officially a business now.

Leo's test horoscopes, then, were quite the turning point, as these would later come to define what most people would understand as astrology. However, astrology, since it was 'fortune-telling', was illegal in the Christian world. By 1912, there were about six to seven hundred fortune-tellers in London and this was a cause for alarm. Astrologers, palmists and clairvoyants were all ordered to remove their signboards from their place of work and halt advertisements. Questions had already been raised in the House of Commons the previous year about the growing menace.

So, when Leo was slapped with two cases, he had to pay a fine for one of them but managed to wriggle out of the other one on the basis of a legal technicality. However, the atmosphere around him was risky and he decided to make some changes. It was at this point that astrology began to metamorphose into a tool of psychological analysis. This would later become the basis of psychological astrology.

But despite the controversial nature of his work, Leo left behind several enduring legacies. First, he domesticated astrology for the first time in human history by taking it to people's homes. One didn't have to seek out an astrologer in person any more for a basic reading and this helped make astrology far more accessible and widely known than it had ever been before. Second, he brought the placement of the Sun in a birth chart to the centre stage. Explaining it in his book, *Esoteric Astrology*, he wrote, 'In the physical man the Sun governs the vital energies and has much significance in connection with the father and the positive side of the nature generally.' Third, he ushered in a New Age astrology which was greatly inspired by theosophy and the Hindu concepts of Karma and reincarnation. His understanding of the latter was influenced by his own research and personal experiences, including two trips to India. Writing in the same book, he remarked, 'On the surface, the Hindu astrologer is apparently a fatalist, but individually he had a firm belief in free will within certain well-defined limits. The very well-established belief in reincarnation and transmigration makes him a fatalist so far as the rewards and punishments of past lives are concerned, and it is to causes set in motion in a former birth that he traces the inevitable fate of the present life; for he has a wider comprehension of the laws of Karma than the Western astrologer.'[5] But while he realised that there was a specific cultural and philosophical context behind the idea of Karma, it didn't stop him from propagating his version of it. Of all his books, *Character Is Destiny*, which focuses on these ideas, still remains his best-known work. This means that Karma, as it was and is perhaps still popularly understood, in the West is quite different than its intended Hindu interpretation.

Leo, then, gave astrology a superficial sense of meaning and profundity that made it ripe for easy obfuscation and commercialisation. Besides Leo, there was also Evangeline Adams in the US. Born in 1868, she was introduced to astrology serendipitously by J. Heber Smith, a Sanskrit scholar and professor of medicine at Boston University.[6] Smith used to employ astrological methods in his medical work and was the one to teach Adams much of what he knew. She had also been attracted to the Hindu Vedanta philosophy after Swami Vivekananda's Chicago speech in 1893. The philosophy, among other things, was rooted in a belief of the cyclicity of life as well as an interconnectedness of life on Earth with the cosmos.[7]

Three years later, she would start her life as an astrologer in New York City when she and her assistant put up at Manhattan's Windsor Hotel under the patronage of its then proprietor, Warren Leland. That year, she predicted a terrible fire accident for the hotel and when it came true, it solidified her position as an astrologer. However, her biographer, Karen Christino, shows that it is possible that Adams never predicted it but was enterprising enough to claim that she had, immediately after the fire broke out.[8] And so, like Leo, her legacy lay in showmanship rather than skill. But both of them were at the forefront of reviving astrology in the UK and in the US respectively.

Working out of a studio she rented at the city's Carnegie Hall, Adams often had high-profile and rich clients, including J.P. Morgan,[9] Joseph Campbell,[10] Charlie Chaplin[11] and many others. In 1930, she became the first astrologer to host a radio show which was broadcast thrice a week, with listeners sending in requests for readings in huge numbers. In addition to that, Adams' sponsors, at one point, would receive four thousand reading requests a day and she employed over twenty-five assistants for her work.[12] She also made predictions for public interest, including the election of Calvin Coolidge as US President in 1924.[13] Like Leo, she too was slapped with cases for 'fortune-telling' and even arrested thrice. But unlike Leo, instead of trying to escape, she fought the trial head on and won it. Bobrick Benson, in *Fated Sky*, notes that 'she came to court armed with reference books, expounded the principles of astrology to the judge at some length and illustrated its practice by reading a blind chart that turned out to be that of the judge's son'. The reading proved to be correct and the judge ruled in her favour, remarking that 'she had raised astrology to the dignity of an exact science' by her work.

Horoscopes Arrive on the Scene

The stage set by Leo and Adams was then occupied by R.H. Naylor and Dane Rudhyar in their respective countries. Naylor started out by accident. *The Daily Express*, one of Britain's most widely circulated newspapers at that time, wanted to do something new for the recently-born Princess Margaret, the daughter of King George VI. The editor, John Gordon, thought it might be a good idea to publish an interpretation of her birth chart and the paper sought to enlist the popular palmist and astrologer Cheiro for the job. But as it turned out, he was too busy, and instead, sent his employee, Naylor, for the job.[14]

The princess was born on 21 August 1930 and the newspaper's sister publication, *Sunday Express*, carried the horoscope three days later. The feature was titled, 'What the Stars Foretell for the New Princess' and predicted an 'eventful' life for the young royal. One specific prediction said that in her seventh year, the royal family and the nation would be impacted by a significant event. That event came to pass when Edward VIII (later the Duke of Windsor) caused a crisis in the country by proposing marriage to an American divorcee. Eventually he had to abdicate the throne and his 326-day-long reign came to an end in December 1936.

However, the horoscope feature captivated the British audience right from day one. To capitalise on their readers' interest, the newspaper decided to repeat it and carried interpretations for those born on each day of a particular week in September 1930 in this new feature. Naylor followed this up with a prediction of a British aircraft accident in October and lo and behold, that came true and cemented his reputation as someone who knew what he was doing. The astrologer was then signed up as a regular and his column came to be known as 'Your Stars'. While he started out with predictions based on birth dates, he switched to the twelve Sun signs in 1937. Such horoscopes were soon being published by many publications across Britain.[15]

Fleeing wartime Europe, Daniel Chennevière, who was born in Paris in 1895, arrived in the United States in 1917. He changed his last name to Rudhyar, fashioned out of Shiva's Rudra form, because he was fascinated by the mythology of Rudra as the god of death, transformation, and rebirth.[16] It was in tune with his personal inclination towards the idea of self-growth that comes from personal challenges. Perhaps he also knew of the Nakshatra of Ardra, which is ruled by Rudra and is indeed a marker of inner turmoil and the resultant emotional growth, as we read before. Like Leo, he also picked up astrology by his association with the theosophists. By 1933, he was writing articles for the magazine *American Astrology* regularly. He suggested the twelve-paragraph daily horoscope version to his editor and the idea was well-received both by his editor as well as the American audience. In time, it became so popular that it was replicated by other publications across the country.

But Rudhyar's true legacy lies in the introduction to astrology, the theory of depth psychology, which looks at the relationship between the conscious and the unconscious in our minds. He remains, to date, the most prolific astrologer who wrote about psychology and astrology. He was inspired by ideas of Carl Gustave Jung in particular and his work revolved around bringing together Jungian psychology to astrology. It caught on well because his work coincided with the New Age movement in Western societies that needed something more than the capitalistic and atheistic way of life. One of his most prominent books, *Practice of Astrology,* was published by Penguin Books in 1970. Other book titles by him include *Astrological Study of Psychological Complexes and Emotional Problems* (1977) and *Astrology of Personality: A Reformulation of Astrological Concepts and Ideals in Terms of Contemporary Psychology and Philosophy* (1987), among others.

By the mid-twentieth century, the face of astrology had changed in the Western world. Traditional and medieval Greek and Islamic astrology had been relegated as a relic of the past. Astrologers did not focus on predictions and were not trying to understand the world around them through planetary movements like their predecessors. Instead, astrology was now about understanding the self and the personality, mostly at a superficial level. In his book *Hindu Astrology and the West,* the renowned Indian astrologer B.V. Raman, on his travels to the United States in 1959, noted that there were close to five thousand astrologers in the country by that time. He described a meeting with one who introduced himself as a psychologist, astrologer and a thought-reader. Raman wrote, '(He) handed over to me a copy of *Your Daily Astrological Guide* (that) was brought out regularly by a publishing firm in the Midwest and (said) that he was connected with several such firms which manufacture such stuff as "Dream Interpretations", "Hollywood Horoscopes", "Stellar Dietetics", and so on.'" He further remarked that while the astrologer claimed he could cast birth charts, his knowledge of predictive astrology was limited to Sun sign readings. When questioned, the astrologer defended himself by saying that 'in order to create serious interest in astrology in the minds of the common public, it was necessary to give them something light and non-technical'. Another astrologer claimed that his investigation into planetary transits revealed how the 'bell-shaped skirts used by women today would give place to a bustle type of skirts by 1970 or so'. According to him, the changes in fashion corresponded to a thirty-six-year cycle of movements of Jupiter and Moon's nodes.'[17]

The Linda Goodman Phenomenon

This initial stage of popularisation of astrology was merely a preamble to Linda Goodman and her book, *Sun Signs*. Published in 1968 in Britain, it became the first ever astrology book to make the *The New York Times* bestseller list. At the time of her death in 1995, her books had sold over thirty million copies in fifteen languages, which was the highest for books on astrology.[18] What she did with her books was nothing short of revolutionary because she personalised the zodiac in a way that had never been done before.

In her introduction to the Sun signs book, she wrote about the importance of analysing a birth chart in entirety to get the full picture of an individual and pointed out how Sun's transits into twelve zodiac signs were not as precise and orderly as most people believed. It is for clarity's sake that even astrologers must pretend otherwise because laypeople cannot be expected to understand such intricacies. Despite this, she believed knowing a person's Sun sign was akin to understanding them more deeply.

The book expanded upon each zodiac sign, with prose that was engaging and fun. With about forty pages dedicated to each sign, it had verses from Lewis Carroll's works introducing each portion. So, if she was writing about how to recognise an Aries person, she quoted Carroll, 'They would not remember the simple rules their friends had taught them, that a red-hot poker will burn you if you hold it too long; and that, if you cut your finger very deeply with a knife, it usually bleeds.' This is followed by a lengthy description that feels like she knows what she's talking about while also being easy to read. In similar fashion, she goes on about various ways in which one encounters an Aries individual.

The Aries man, then, is a 'natural rebel' who thinks he was born smarter than the rest of the world, and for that reason, 'those in more powerful positions will teach him frequent lessons in humility' and a woman who can handle his shattered ego with love and compassion gets to have him forever. The Aries woman, on the other hand, is likened to *Gone With the Wind*'s Scarlett O'Hara, and like her, Mars women are 'tough enough to defy convention, face an advancing army or even shoot a man through the head with icy calmness, if he threatens her loved ones'. In this way, the Aries child, employee and boss are also described. The pattern is repeated for all the twelve signs, each of them treated with similar wit and prose.

In her book *Love Signs*, published in 1978, every chapter was preceded by verses from J.M. Barrie's *Peter Pan*, much like her previous book. The Aries Lover, then, was literally an infant in love as the first sign of the zodiac. This individual was here to teach his or her partner the innocence of love while they had to learn the lesson of trusting people. Goodman then explores compatibilities of an Aries lover with all the twelve zodiac signs. This incredibly detailed, creatively interpretative and public-friendly way of looking at Sun signs took off like nothing else before. This was also a decisive departure from astrology's image as a tradition that, like all traditions, could be orthodox, ridiculous and a superstition of the past. Her model of astrology, even more popular than what Leo, Naylor and Rudhyar did, was replicated in publications across the world, and soon it would become impossible to find any newspaper or magazine that didn't carry daily, weekly and monthly predictions for Sun signs. These predictions were not always based on regular inputs from actual astrologers and were more creative writing than astrology.

But what made the system of 'Sun Signs' so enduring? For one, these were far easier to popularise than birth chart astrology. One could now have an element of the spiritual or the psychological without getting their feet dirty. But more importantly, this was due to a phenomenon known as the Barnum Effect. The term was coined by Paul Meehl, an American psychologist, in the 1950s. According to him, vague personality descriptions or statements felt accurate to people because of what their brains did subconsciously—fill up the material with real details that only they were privy to. This, many believe, explains the popularity of Sun sign horoscopes. While reading about these Sun signs were harmless fun most of the times, the mainstreaming of these ended up being counterproductive. Not only did a market emerge out of this, many 'believers' also tend to excuse their bad or unhealthy behaviour by blaming it on their Sun sign. This is akin to perpetuating ignorance over and over again because most people still do not understand the distinction between these Sun signs and astrology. While this has prevented many from looking at astrology critically, there have been some in the past who have taken up that mantle.

Notes

1   Bobrick Benson, *Fated Sky: Astrology in History* (Simon and Schuster, 2006), pp. 266-268 and Kim Farnell, *A Brief Biography of Alan Leo* (Skyscript, 2006), https://www.skyscript.co.uk/Alan_Leo.html.

2   Suzanne Scott, 'What is the Age of Aquarius and What

Does It Mean for You' (*Vogue*, 2021), https://www.vogue.in/culture-and-living/content/according-to-astrology-the-age-of-aquarius-is-coming-this-is-what-it-means-for-you.

3   Nicholas Campion, *Astrology and Cosmology in World's Religions* (NYU Press, 2012), p. 193.

4   Kim Farnell, *A Brief Biography of Alan Leo* (Skyscript, 2006), https://www.skyscript.co.uk/Alan_Leo.html.

5   Alan Leo, *Esoteric Astrology* (Modern Astrology, 1913), p. 35.

6   Karen Christino, *Foreseeing the Future: Evangeline Adams and Astrology in America* (Stella Mira Books, 2019), pp. 32-34.

7   Ibid., p. 48.

8   Ibid., pp. 7-8.

9   Ibid., p. 75.

10 Ibid., p. 159.

11 Ibid., p. 149.

12 Ibid., p. 189.

13 Ibid., p. 150.

14 Bobrick Benson, *Fated Sky: Astrology in History* (Simon and Schuster, 2006), p. 274.

15 Elena Nicolaou, 'Why Doesn't The Crown Show How Princess Margaret Helped Create Modern Astrology' (*Oprah Daily*, 2019), https://www.oprahdaily.com/entertainment/tv-movies/a29834847/princess-margaret-horoscope-astrology-history-the-crown/.

16 Sanaa Taha, *Wheels Within Wheels: A Critical Biography of Dane Rudhyar* (Spica: Postgraduate Journal for Cosmology of Culture, 2014), https://www.academia.edu/9087106/Wheels_within_Wheels_A_Critical_Biography_of_Dane_Rudhyar.

17 B.V. Raman, *Hindu Astrology and the West* (UBS Publishers' Distributors, 1992), pp. 133-134.

18 *The Spokesman Review*, '"Sun Signs" Author Linda Goodman Dies', 1995, https://www.spokesman.com/stories/1995/oct/25/sun-signs-author-linda-goodman-dies/.

11

Popularising Astrology:
Carl Jung and B.V. Raman

After the likes of Leo and Linda Goodman propounded a pop version of astrology, it brought astrology back into the mainstream after being on the sidelines for a couple of centuries. And when that happened, thinkers and astrologers alike ventured into the depths of it once again. They did so out of curiosity about aspects of human life, but also as a life mission.

Born in 1875 in Switzerland, the Swiss psychoanalyst Carl Gustave Jung was probably the most influential individual in the Western world in the last century to have explored astrology. His legacy lies in bringing astrology into the mould of psychology, which opened up many frontiers for the former. He famously proclaimed at one point, 'whatever is born or done at this particular moment of time has the quality of this moment of time', explaining that there was too much coincidence in the appearance of certain thoughts, symbols, and psychic conditions in life.

Jung started his career with a fruitful professional association with the Austrian-born Dr Sigmund Freud, founder of the psychoanalytic method. But the protégé soon eclipsed the mentor in fame, for his ideas were relevant and digestible to the general public as well. Differences in approach caused them to split up, after which Jung went on to create his own body of work—most importantly, the theory of the collective unconscious and archetypes. He explored the psyche through these archetypes, which he believed were universal in nature and showed up in cultures across the world.

The collective unconscious bears a striking resemblance to the concept of Brahman and Atman, which is described in the Hindu texts of the Upanishads. According to Jung, the individual psyche was influenced by not just one's own subconscious or unconscious workings but that of the entire world's, which is what was termed the collective unconscious.

Psyche as the Basis for Astrology

In his book, *Man and His Symbols*, he explained it in detail, 'Goethe's *Faust* aptly says, "*Im Anfang war die Tat*", or, in the beginning was the deed. "Deeds" were never invented, they were done; thoughts on the other hand, are a relatively late discovery of man. First he was moved to deeds by unconscious factors; it was only a long time afterwards that he began to reflect upon the causes that had moved him; and it took him a very long time indeed to arrive at the preposterous idea that he must have moved himself—his mind being unable to identify any other motivating force than his own.' Jung concluded, then, that the human psyche was highly subject to the unconscious processes within. This was, in fact, true of plants and animals as well, even if they possessed a lower level of consciousness than humans. Until the medieval times and in some parts of the world even today, aspects of this unconscious were represented in Gods, Goddesses, demons, spirits, mythical stories and so on since the advent of humanity—whatever was out there was there because it was within. These figures had all the elements of what it means to be human, from the best to the most grotesque. However, this was done to be in constant awareness of one's inner realities and to confront them whenever the need arose. This was a more natural way of life and even helped mitigate one's occasional disruptive tendencies.[1]

According to Jung, modern society's problem was two-fold. In abandoning religion and myth, not only had it lost a way of confronting one's psychological complexes but it had also forgotten the importance of psyche itself. While humanity was obsessed with understanding and controlling nature, it paid little attention to what Jung believed was the essence of a human being—the psyche. It was here that our complex and unfamiliar impulses and compulsions originated. He wrote, 'Man's greatest instrument, his psyche, is little thought of, and it is often directly mistrusted and despised. "It's only psychological" too often means: It is nothing.'[2]

He believed that as long as humans were subject to their unconscious tendencies, which could manifest as difficult to understand emotions and sudden mood swings, their conscious decisions were not all that conscious. They were not their own masters, and one of the ways to understand these unconscious processes was through archetypes. The collective unconscious was a storehouse of the stories of humans that came before us, and patterns in those stories gave rise to archetypes. The archetypes identified by Jung included that of the hero, the trickster, the child, the wise old man, the orphan, and more.

As a psychologist, he rejected the notion of a human being born as a blank slate, or a tabula rasa. One's unconscious carried one's inherent archetypal tendencies that ended up shaping their lives, whether they realised it or not. The goal of human life, then, was to become aware of these archetypal influences and go through what is known as individuation process in Jungian psychology. Individuation, in his opinion, was the process by which an individual attained full potential as a result of greater self-awareness. It made one more authentic, free to act without being held back by one's psychological complexes.

In this way, the collective unconscious was akin to Hinduism's Brahman, and the individualised person was the Atman. But while in the Hindu conception the Atman is supposed to cease complete identification with the ego in order to merge with the Brahman to attain Moksha, Jung's self-realised individual could not actually do that. In fact, that was pretty much a 'psychic death' according to him.[3] But it was this process of individuation that became the principle of psychological astrology, propounded by later astrologers who were inspired by Jungian psychology.

Synchronicity and Astrology

Jung's idea of astrology was not directly related to individuation. He was instead fascinated by apparent correlation between one's conscious and what manifested in one's external world. He called this synchronicity, using the term for the first time in 1930 while explaining *I Ching* to an audience.[4] The seed for this theory of 'meaningful coincidences' had been sown in him while he was still quite young, and he wanted to boil down the magical, the fantastical and superstitious into something that could be understood empirically. As a psychologist dealing primarily in psychotic disorders, it was perhaps natural for him to take a deep dive into the human subconscious. For this, he often turned to Eastern thought, even though he was also wary of it because he felt it was fundamentally incompatible with the way the Western mind was structured.

Other than this, he was also buoyed by parapsychologist J.B. Rhine's statistical analysis of psychokinetic experiments in which participants would guess the number and sign of a playing card before it was shown to them. Every participant had to do this eight hundred times and the average probability of getting a correct answer was deemed to be five correct answers for every twenty-five cards. The results, however, showed an average of 6.5 correct answers for every twenty-five cards. The probability of this deviation was one out of 250,000. This was encouraging, and so, the researchers decided to take it to the next level.

In the next phase of it, the spatial distance between the participant and the experimenter was increased to different distances. In one case, it was four hundred kilometres. Asked to guess the card now, a participant was now able to get a correct answer ten times for every twenty-five cards. In later stages of this experiment, similar results were seen even when the participant sat in one country and the experimenter in another.[5] Now while all of it could be chalked up to chance, it was fascinating for Jung. He thought it pointed to a deeper reality of the unconscious and its manifestations in the material world.

He also borrowed, for his intuition, from the German philosopher Arthur Schopenhauer, who believed there was a common denominator to omens, presage and astrology. Schopenhauer, in fact, seemed to believe in fate as well, for he once wrote, '... when you reach an advanced age and look back over your lifetime, it can seem to have had a consistent order and plan, as though composed by some novelist. Events that when they occurred had seemed accidental and of little moment turn out to have been indispensable factors in the composition of a consistent plot'.[6] He believed that one's fate was composed within one's consciousness, of which one usually remained unaware for most part. This must have been on Jung's mind when he claimed that until one made their unconscious conscious, it would manifest in one's external world in a way that feels like fate.

Synchronicity, in his view, then, was a 'psychically conditioned relativity of space and time ... in relation to psyche, space and time are elastic and can apparently be reduced almost to vanishing point, as though they were dependent on psychic conditions and did not exist in themselves but were only "postulated" by the conscious mind'. He was convinced that he was onto something because '[these apparent] "coincidences" were connected so meaningfully that their "chance" concurrence would represent a degree of improbability that would have to be expressed by an astronomical figure'. Archetypes were the way in which synchronicity manifested itself in our lives by shaping our characters and life events. The more individualised one was with one's archetypal tendencies, the more clearly one could perceive synchronicities in one's life. Synchronicity, then, was nothing more than one's subconscious speaking to one's conscious through dreams, apparently random events, and more.[7]

Jung had witnessed many instances from his life as well as that of his patients that convinced him of these ideas. He felt that the scientific community needed to redefine how it understood space and time as well as the unconscious in order to truly understand what is going on around us. In order to put his theory to test, he conducted an experiment of his own. He gathered a total of 966 horoscopes of married couples and looked at astrological combinations for these 483 marriages. There were several overlaps between a couple's horoscopes, such as Sun–Moon, Moon–Moon, and Moon-ascendant conjunctions, in line with traditional astrological principles.[8] However, as Jung himself admitted, the results of the experiment did not prove the case for astrology as decisively as he had hoped it would.

He explained it away by remarking that it was difficult, and perhaps impossible, to verify the synchronistic phenomena. He believed that even though the modern West had by and large done away with all sorts of superstitions, it had not been able to do away with astrology. It was through psychology and parapsychology, he wrote in the conclusion of his book on synchronicity, that there emerged a model to study the physical side of psychic events. Despite the obvious difficulties of such a study, he was convinced that it was absolutely needed.

These ideas of archetypes and synchronicity also inspired a generation of thinkers and writers after Jung. From the noted Czech psychotherapist Stanislav Grof to the American writer Joseph Campbell, many have resonated with these concepts time and again. In fact, for Campbell, they informed much of his life's work. A phrase by him, 'follow your bliss', inspired by the Sanskrit phrase, 'Sat-Chit-Ananda', became so popular that it has since influenced countless college students in the US, and also the likes of Star Wars creator George Lucas and writer Dan Brown. He explained the reasoning behind it in his book Power of Myth (1988) as, '... we must be willing to let go of the life we planned so as to have the life that is waiting for us', which sounds quite astrological in nature. Archetypal myths, he believed, served as an extremely important device in navigating one's life; for in the journeys of our lives it is apt if we think of ourselves as the hero or the heroine. Walking this heroic path, we meet many obstacles and therein lies our transformation and liberation. The more we walk the path of our lives, the closer we get to our bliss or God. While it fits in very well with a secular worldview, it is essentially a reiteration of not only Jung's but also the astrological idea of aligning closely to one's inherent personality and purpose. Archetypal myths help make this process more personal and poetic.

Jung's work as a psychoanalyst also led to the development of what is known as the Myers–Briggs Type Indicator or MBTI, which can be understood as astrology for corporates. Like astrology, it divides people into sixteen possible types, and measures aspects such as extroversion vs introversion, sensing vs intuition, thinking vs feeling, and finally, perceiving vs judging. This model was developed by an American woman, Katharine Cook–Briggs, because she wanted to understand the best way to raise her daughter, Isabel Briggs Myers. She relied on Jung's theory that factors such as sensing, intuition, feeling and thinking were dominant in an individual at a given point of time and that is how they navigated their daily life. So, even though it has nothing to do with the astrological ideas of Jung, it functions as a form of psychological astrology.

While Jung later sought to dissociate his work and his publicly expressed views on astrology, he is often credited by astrologers for making astrology respectable. In fact, in a letter dated 26 May 1954 to a Mr Barbault, he wrote of his thoughts on synchronicity, astrology and psychology.[9] He took umbrage with astrologers, saying that they did not consider their interpretations to be mere possibilities and could be too literal rather than being symbolic with them. The planets and the zodiac, according to Jung, did not, in and by themselves, do anything, but were impersonal and objective facts. There were several 'layers of meaning' that should be taken into account while conducting an astrological interpretation. But despite this annoyance, he said that 'astrology has much to offer psychology, but what the latter can offer its elder sister is less evident'. He believed that both could learn something from the other as both were about recognising, understanding and interpreting archetypes and symbols that pervade the daily human life.

B.V. Raman's Mission

A few years prior to this, the renowned Indian astrologer B.V. Raman too had sought Jung's views on astrology[10] and on conducting a statistical analysis of horoscopes. This was in 1943, and Jung mentioned how useful he found it to read his patients' birth charts, writing, 'I must say that I very often found that the astrological data elucidated certain points which I otherwise would have been unable to understand.' He continued, 'From such experiences, I formed the opinion that astrology is of particular interest to the psychologist, since it contains a sort of psychological experience which we call "projected"—this means that we find the psychological facts, as it were, in the constellations. This originally gave rise to the idea that these factors derive from the stars, whereas they are merely in a relation of synchronicity with them ... What I miss in astrological literature is chiefly the statistical method by which certain fundamental facts could be scientifically established.'

While Raman found the psychological application of astrology fascinating, he later changed his views about looking at astrology statistically. He felt, as many astrologers do, that the ability to predict correctly was a matter of experience and intuition and that a scientific study of such a discipline was, by definition, impossible. But he was surprised by the popularity of psychological astrology. In his memoirs, he mentioned meeting the wife of a European diplomat in Delhi who told him how many psychoanalysts and psychiatrists in the United States were 'applied astrologers'. While these professionals never disclosed this publicly, out of fear of losing their medical licences, they made liberal use of astrology to diagnose the mental issues of their patients. He found this to be true when he visited the States himself and interacted with various such doctors. A Chicago-based psychologist, for instance, told him that he found a correlation between different mental disorders and afflictions of Mercury, the planet of intellect, in a birth chart. That was not a surprise to Raman because according to Jyotish, Mercury's interactions with the Moon, Mars, Saturn and the Nodes did indeed reflect mental afflictions such as obsessional neurosis, delusions, dissociation and false beliefs.[11]

He felt that Indians had not been able to develop a psychological brand of astrology because the people believed in Karma more than anything else. In his book, *Hindu Astrology and the West*, he wrote, 'In the West, psychosis and neurosis have been claiming a large number of victims because of the peculiar social and industrial conditions there. It is, therefore, understandable that Western astrologers, in order to tackle problems peculiar to their civilisation, have been successful in developing psychological astrology to considerable perfection. We can with advantage import these findings and adapt them to our own needs.' This was an astute observation, for even Jung believed that the Western society's disconnect and suppression of the natural way of life, where the human was able to confront the darker aspects of his psyche through mythical deities, was the reason for the modern man's neurosis.

But where Jung was instrumental in establishing modern psychological astrology, B.V. Raman's work was perhaps even more important in the revival of Jyotish both in India and elsewhere. B.V. Raman, or Bangalore Venkata Raman, was born in 1912. The prefix Bangalore was due to the fact that Raman's family had lived there for over 350 years after his Brahmin ancestor, Saranavarjulu, migrated from Andhra Pradesh to Bangalore after the collapse of the Vijayanagar Empire in search of patronage and earning a livelihood. His grandfather, B. Suryanarain Rao, was an accomplished astrologer who wrote books, delivered lectures on the topic and practised astrology for sixty years. Alan Leo had met him while on his travels to India and it was through his grandfather that Raman knew of him.[12] Rao had set the young Raman on the path to astrology and taught him the first couple of verses when he was eight. He had predicted from his grandson's birth chart that he would one day become well-known around the world, and Raman intentionally pursued that fame and greatness.

By the time he was fourteen, he knew a few texts on astrology by heart and tried predicting the time of death of all his family members. For this, he was chided by Rao who warned him that such a prediction required a careful examination of a horoscope and he was too young and immature to do that at that age anyway. Raman, in his memoirs, admits to being egoistical about his knowledge and skills as an astrologer when he was young and how his grandfather constantly had to cut him to size to keep him grounded. At the age of eighteen, he wanted to revive his grandfather's magazine, *The Astrological Magazine*, that the latter had launched in 1895. But because he did not put out issues regularly and published an issue once every two to three years, it never really took off.

For the next six years, Raman got around fifty people to subscribe to it and pooled together financial resources to finally relaunch it in 1936. Amongst his supporters was the proprietor of *The Hindu*, Kasturi Srinivasan.[13] While he was reluctant, he pledged a hundred rupees to him as a donation and promised to help him publicise the magazine and his work in the newspaper. In his opening editorial, Raman wrote, '*The Astrological Magazine* has been the only organ, throughout India and the foreign countries, which has been successfully ventilating the grievances under which its professors are placed. It is the only journal which deals with astrological matters in a scientific and popular way. We propose to continue the useful task of reviving astrology and other ancient Indian sciences and place before the scientific and educated world ...' The magazine had sections like Astrology for Beginners, Elements of Astronomy, columns for discussing controversial astrological questions, new interpretations from old and existing astrological texts, and more. He remained the chief editor of the magazine for the next sixty-two years, i.e., until his death in 1998. During this time, he also wrote around fifteen books on astrology, including *My Experiences in Astrology* and *Hindu Astrology and the West.*

In addition to being a prolific writer, he was enthusiastic about spreading awareness about Jyotish. In his travels to the West in the 1960s, he visited places like New York, Washington, Boston, Chicago, Los Angeles, London, Berlin, Austria, Amsterdam, Rome, Athens, Japan, and more. He'd lecture at astrological associations and lodges but also meet people from other walks of life—scientists, ambassadors, reporters, and so on. He also visited the United Nations and in an informal discussion with four diplomats from Europe, India, Egypt and South America, spoke about astrology. A European diplomat, evidently an amateur astrologer himself, presented his theory of how tensions in international relations corresponded to Uranus–Saturn–Jupiter movements.[14] Raman himself felt that the UN had been created under inauspicious influences as '[its] horoscope mirrors the distrust and intolerance of the nations composing the body. The Saturn–Mars conjunction, which is at the base of power politics between the Western democracies and the communist countries, will further increase the ever-darkening fog of distrust. The UN is bound to go the way of League of Nations.' The day after this he met V.K. Krishna Menon, one of the most influential Indian politicians of his time.[15] At this time, he was the chairman of the Indian delegation of the UN General Assembly as well as the defence minister of India. Meeting at Menon's hotel, Raman described him as being agitated after a 'rub with late General Thimmayya and was feeling uneasy that he might be required to quit'. Examining his horoscope, Raman told him that he wouldn't need to do that but 'his Waterloo would come only in 1962, when according to me, as a consequence of the eighth planet combination, China was likely to commit aggression against India'. Menon was happy to be relieved of his ongoing anxiety but was sceptical about a socialist country doing something like that. The predictions about Menon quitting, and aggression by China, unfortunately, did come true and the resulting war was a huge strain on India's resources as well as the morale of the leaders at the time, including Prime Minister Nehru's.

Years later, in 1968, the Burmese diplomat, U. Thant, sought him out as well.[16] In his first term as UN Secretary General, Thant had helped negotiate talks between the US president John F. Kennedy and the Soviet leader Nikita

Khrushchev during the Cuban Missile Crisis of 1962. He did not wish to pursue another term and so, tendered his resignation from the position. However, as he was being let go, he wanted to know Raman's assessment. The latter wrote back, 'Even if you have made up your mind to sign, Jupiterian influences in your chart are such that you will be obliged to continue for another term.' Thant ended up withdrawing the resignation and served another term during which he criticised the US for the Vietnam War and oversaw the entry of many African and Asian nations into the UN. He did indeed refuse to serve a third term.

Raman, in his travels and writing, perhaps fulfilled his grandfather's prediction about his life. In 1984, he set up the Indian Council of Astrological Sciences (ICAS) with the goal of establishing a pan-India body of astrologers. It conducts various one- and two-year programmes in astrology, palmistry and Vastu Shastra. Its chapters are spread across fifteen of India's twenty-eight states.

But where Jung and Raman lit the candle, the flaming torch of reviving and adapting traditional astrology to the modern times had yet to be taken up. This took place towards the end of the twentieth century.

Notes

1   Carl Jung, *Man and His Symbols* (Dell Publishing, 1968), pp. 70-71.
2   Ibid., p. 93.
3   Ryan Smith, 'How Indian Philosophy Influenced Jung' (IDR Labs, 2014), https://www.idrlabs.com/articles/2014/11/how-indian-philosophy-influenced-jung/.

4   Carl Jung, *Synchronicity* (Princeton University Press, 1973), p. 8 of Editorial Preface.

5   Ibid., p. 17.

6   Ibid., p. 13.

7   Ibid., pp. 19-20.

8   Ibid., p. 46.

9   *Letters of C.G Jung: Volume 1 (1906-1950), Letter on Astrology* (Routledge, 1973), https://carljungdepthpsychologysite. blog/2020/06/23/carl-jungs-letter-on-astrology-3/#. YXpzlp5Bw2x.

10   B.V. Raman, *My Experiences in Astrology* (UBS Publishers, 1992), p. 313.

11   B.V. Raman, *Hindu Astrology and the West* (UBS Publishers, 1992), pp. 139-140.

12   B.V. Raman, *My Experiences in Astrology* (UBS Publishers, 1992), p. 61.

13   Ibid., p. 170.

14   B.V. Raman, *Hindu Astrology and the West* (UBS Publishers, 1992), p. 92.

15   Ibid., p. 94.

16   Ibid., p. 199.

12

Reforming Astrology:
The Three Roberts and the Rao

After the popularisation of Sun signs and a celebrated psychoanalyst's experiments with astrology came the true revivalists in the Western world—the three Roberts. These were Robert Hand, Robert Zoller and Robert Schmidt. They came together for what is known as Project Hindsight and worked on translating medieval astrological texts into English. The venture began in 1993 and among its aims were to reconstruct the practice of Hellenistic astrology, uncover the theoretical foundation behind the discipline and trace the transmission of these ideas through the centuries. Some of the texts translated by them include

Ptolemy's *Tetrabiblos*, Vettius Valens' works, fragments of Antiochus' thesaurus, and more. Hand and Zoller, however, soon parted ways with Schmidt who worked on Project Hindsight until 1996.

Despite the short association, each of the three Roberts made a substantial contribution towards reviving the practice of traditional astrology in the West today. Each of these men came from a different background but they shared a common goal of rescuing astrology from its obscurity of the past few centuries. Each of them took a unique approach towards astrology, solving its problems in their own ways. All three were born between 1940 and 1950 in the US; Zoller and Schmidt passed away a few years ago while Hand continues to work towards the revival of astrology.

Unlike his namesakes, Robert Schmidt didn't start out as an astrologer. He studied Greek and Renaissance Mathematics at college and continued to pursue it thereafter. His primary interest was in translating old manuscripts and texts into English, which were published through the press set up by him and his wife, Ellen Black, in 1985. This press, Golden Hind Press, would soon prove to be instrumental in another way.

After running into an astrologer at a conference in 1989, Schmidt became interested in exploring the astrological texts of Hellenistic Egypt. He discussed his ideas in detail in his paper, 'Problem of Astrology', in 2000.[1] Believing the Greek tradition to be the basis of all Western traditions, he wanted to understand the Greek texts because he felt that 'Greek principles and Greek thinking [were] always pulling our strings in ways that we are not always aware of'. For that, he wanted to understand the texts in the context of their time, draw whatever he could to modern times and then do away with those texts once and for all. And he considered the 'problem of astrology' to be one of the most persistent problems, calling it an 'itch that consciousness has never been able to satisfactorily scratch' since its advent in the Western world two thousand years ago. He found astrology to be incompatible with modern civilisation, yet felt that in its genesis lay answers to most of our philosophical and metaphysical inquiry. Labelling astrology a 'repository or point of accumulation for everything we don't know', he believed that the field existed in the shadow of science because it was the dumping ground of all that science was not yet willing to come to terms with.

In order to undertake that investigation, he thought that it was important to define astrology as the ancients understood it, rather than go by our modern-day definitions. Failing to do so would seriously impair the outcome of such a task, he cautioned. Like a true philosopher, he wrote, 'Modern astrologers often like to think of astrology as a symbolic language of the stars, a divine language, and I believe ancient astrologers would also have approved of this characterization. But shouldn't this celestial grammar, this celestial logic, then be the standard for our human languages? And may it not be the case that the stars are trying to teach us the proper use of logos, of language? Wouldn't it then follow that only the proper use of argumentation and dialectical inquiry will provide us access to the problem of astrology itself?'

Schmidt also thought that in studying astrology, one could understand the limitations and vulnerabilities of all modern disciplines such as physics, philosophy and psychology. In his final analysis, he considered the 'problem of astrology' to be an exploration that was born out of a love for wisdom, for astrology itself was connected to wisdom.

Where Schmidt brought in a love for ancient wisdom and philosophy to the table, Zoller brought in a love for tradition and technique. He studied Latin at college and to his German father's dismay, began reading tarot cards quite early on in his youth. He went on to work odd jobs to sustain himself before he took up astrology seriously. Even then, he continued to run a construction-related business for the most part of his life. But as an astrologer, he ushered in a revolution in the West.[2]

Post the 1950s, modern Western astrology had become all about looking into the outer planets, Neptune, Uranus and Pluto, even though these three were not discovered until 1930 and so were never a part of traditional astrology. The influences of these planets were considered to be psychological, which was in line with the increasing popularity of Sun signs as well as a focus on the psyche while reading a birth chart. For astrologers of this persuasion, there wasn't much to astrology before the likes of Alan Leo.

It was Zoller, then, who brought a greater awareness about what astrology truly was, by bringing medieval astrology to public consciousness. His first book, *The Arabic Parts: A Lost Key to Prediction*, published in 1989, drew on techniques from Arabic astrology that had not been used in the Western world since at least the seventeenth century. Believing New Age astrology to be a degeneration of medieval astrology, he would force his students to focus on the traditional functions of astrology, such as making accurate predictions. He would, for instance, tell them to predict their date of death, which was a shock to many of his students because that wasn't how they were trained to look at astrology. He remained a lifelong proponent of medieval astrology and is widely credited for bringing a seriousness to the practice of traditional astrology in the West in recent decades.

Traditional Versus New Age Astrology

Zoller found the New Age conception of astrology, whose direction was partly due to Carl Jung, to be untenable. He didn't like its secularisation, demystification and reduction to the psyche. As a Catholic, he instead believed astrology to be an indication of the God's will. The personal will, therefore, was largely irrelevant when pitted against that of God's and astrology was meant to help us understand where to direct our efforts. He was also disdainful of the contemporary West's tendency to reduce everything down to logic and mathematics in order to eschew even a modicum of spirituality. At the same time, however, he was suspicious of people who 'think this problem of how unmanifest "energies" which flow from the heart become astrological influences and ultimately become embodied in natural things has been solved'. In other words, he felt that there was definitely something to astrology that helped one fulfil the divine destiny but it wasn't yet a fully-developed perfect system. He believed in using intuition and was deeply sceptical of developing computer software to make predictions.[3]

The third of the Roberts, Robert Hand, remains one of the most influential figures of astrology in the West today. He studied history at college and that still informs a lot of his work as an astrologer. He started out as a full-time astrologer in 1972 and after the split with Project Hindsight, he set up ARHAT or the Archive for the Retrieval of Historical Astrological Texts. The organisation is involved in researching and publishing astrological texts and manuscripts, possibly the only such widespread initiative in the West today. He has written several books on astrology and served on many international astrological associations. He is also a former chairman of the board of Kepler College, one of the few educational institutions to study astrology in the US. Unlike Zoller, Hand was an early adopter of technology as an astrologer and was one of the first people to write astrology software. His most notable venture is Astrolabe, which was started by him as Astro-Graphics Services in 1979.

Also, unlike Zoller, he isn't too sceptical of Jungian thought because he thinks that despite being a modern man, Jung thought like an occultist, and cites the success of MBTI as a validation of the psychoanalyst's methods. He isn't averse to using psychology in astrology or looking at techniques from other astrological systems.

Hand doesn't believe in managing every aspect of his life through astrology but finds value in looking at transits and understanding how they play out in one's life. An example he often shares is one of a birth chart reading he did back in 1998 where the client was supposed to have had a difficult year mentally, which included an indication of possible drug use. However, when he enquired about it, it turned out that the client had actually made over a million dollars and played the character of Judy Garland in a musical. Garland was a hugely popular Hollywood actress who led a tragic personal life and died of a drug overdose in 1969 at the age of forty-seven. The transits, then, it appeared, manifested in the client's life through the performance rather than her own personal life. For Hand, this validated the astrological principle that the planets are not inherently malefic but the way people tend to experience certain influences makes them negative. This is particularly relevant because Saturn and Mars, the two big malefics, are the cause of much alarm and superstition in much of the astrological practice around the world.[4]

But while Hand has been more progressive than most astrologers, he gives the tradition the respect he thinks it deserves. He explains, '... the most common allegation made about traditional astrology is that it is fatalistic and not oriented towards human potential. I've actually found, from studying ancient philosophy as applied to astrology, that this philosophy gives the only system which has a solid philosophical rationale for human potential. Modern astrology just does it by wishful thinking or by varyingly appropriate or inappropriate applications of depth-psychology through astrology. But the ancient material has it built into the astrology.' He cites the Greek philosopher Aristotle to support the belief that life is about self-actualisation and astrology can help with that.

In this way, the three managed to revive traditional astrology in the modern West and adapt it to not just the latest technology but thought as well. It is significant because this revival comes after centuries of astrology going through its ups and downs and eventually being sidelined as ridiculous superstition. That it came after the tabloid-like popularity of Sun signs says something about astrology itself—it will always be sought out by humanity but will more likely be misused and misappropriated at the mass level. People will always want to know about the future or understand themselves in the context of the cosmos but both endeavours will likely fail for the most part. At the same time, there will always be select individuals who will want to delve deep into astrology and unearth the gems underneath the mud.

K.N. Rao and Teaching Astrology

What the three Roberts did for the West, K.N. Rao did for India and Jyotish. But where the former brought back tradition to a modern society, the latter modernised it through research and education in a still-traditional society. Rao was born to a former journalist, K. Rama Rao, and astrologer, K. Saraswani Devi, in October 1931 in the southern state of Andhra Pradesh in India. However, he grew up in the north Indian city of Lucknow, giving him the opportunity to mix with people from diverse communities early on in life—something he feels he could not have experienced if he had grown up around the 'extreme Brahminical orthodoxy of south Indian society of those days'. At the age of eleven, when he fell ill with typhoid, his mother initiated him into astrology, numerology and palmistry, and started teaching him in the hopes of helping him get better.[5] He went on to join the Indian Audit and Accounts Service, after a stint as an English lecturer in 1957, and worked his way up to the post of director-general by the time of his retirement in November 1990.

While Rao had often consulted for friends, family and acquaintances as a service, astrology remained in the background of his life well into the 1980s. Things changed after he met his Jyotish guru, Swami Vidyaranya of Bihar, who called himself Moorkhanandji. The guru told Rao that he should never give up astrology as even though it was presently in disrepair, he would become the reason of its revival.[6] That prophecy would manifest itself in a few years when an educational course in Jyotish was introduced at New Delhi's Bhartiya Vidya Bhawan in association with B.V. Raman's ICAS. The course, introduced on 14 August 1987 at 10.50 a.m., was inaugurated by Arjun Singh, the then cabinet minister of communication.[7] But the course did not get off to a smooth start—the second batch saw only one student appear for the examinations out of over twenty. When the remaining students were questioned about their no-show, they claimed that they were not confident of clearing the exams as the teaching had been vague and incomprehensible. To correct this, Rao decided to take on classes while still working a full-time job.

But this was not enough. Raman maintained a tight hold over many aspects of the course—hiring of teachers, assigned books, and so on. Rao would often come up against him, voicing his opposition to Raman's methods and manoeuvres. Eventually, by 1994, there was a proper crisis and the course administration decided to sever all connections with ICAS. Now it was Rao who would go on to spearhead the course's future. His two main legacies in the revival of Jyotish are opening up the study of astrology to all, irrespective of their caste, religion, gender and age, and research into Jyotish in order to make astrological principles relevant to the modern age. Both of these were significant changes to effect in India as there was a lot of orthodoxy and resistance to change when it came to Jyotish.

Where formerly one had to be initiated in the study of Jyotish by a guru who was usually a Brahmin priest, Rao made it a point to open it up for everyone. The classes are conducted over the weekends and the experience resembles more of a university classroom than the traditional setup where one is taught by a guru and learns it as a spiritual practice.

But the real game-changer was the idea that the astrological texts had to be reinterpreted according to the changing times. When India opened up its economy in 1991, it ushered in cultural changes that the sages of ancient India could never have foreseen. Within a few years, there were jobs that no one had heard of before. Large scale vehicle ownership and air travel were becoming increasingly common. More women started working full-time, sustaining both their job and the household at the same time. Many households had a computer now and more children were growing up in nuclear families as opposed to joint families. The metro cities would soon become so advanced that parts of it would feel like a foreign world to someone from a tier 2 city a few hundred kilometres away. In other words, traditional Indian society was becoming modern in a Western sense. But even though most of these Indians would still consult astrologers, regular astrologers hadn't revised their interpretations in centuries. In fact, most of these astrologers still mechanically parrot generations-old interpretations.

Rao claims that while old texts cannot address the modern society, astrological principles are 'eternally valid'. He believes that research into astrology should never stop, for as society is ever-changing, it would have no utility otherwise if it did not stay current. For the orthodox priest, he has nothing but contempt—'Forget the obscurantist pandit who puts a very narrow meaning of the sutra. He does this terrible sutra chopping and confuses you. I call them "sutra-chopping" pandits. They put one meaning of the sutra stupidly, and then they say, "No, it cannot be anything else!" I say to them, "Apply it and show me the results." But they just cannot show the results. They don't know how to interpret the sutras, apply it, and produce research. They'll only quote texts.'[8]

According to Rao, even reading translations of astrological texts is 'the art of picking up gems from undeclared dung heaps' to form a coherent perspective of an astrological principle. For example, if the texts mention that the cause of one's death would be a vulture, then its modern interpretation would be that one would be shot to death by an assassin. Rao claims that on the basis of this, he was able to predict Indian Prime Minister Indira Gandhi's death, who was shot and killed by her bodyguard.[9] Similarly, when it comes to marriage-related predictions, the texts mention one's future life partner's possible caste or a traditional ancient occupation such as that of an ironsmith or a warrior, and so on. But since today one can be a farmer as well as a social media activist, it is the astrologer's intelligence and exposure to the modern world that becomes more important than the texts.

Bhartiya Vidya Bhavan's astrology course students have been conducting research into various aspects of life such as finance, marriage, profession, education, diseases, and so on. These research studies are published by the department in their bi-monthly *Journal of Astrology*, both in English and Hindi. Each research article includes an analysis of twenty horoscopes to explain a particular trend such as what might make one a journalist, what causes cancer, what may lead to a tragic death, indications of a broken relationship, what might indicate a career in an airline, and so on. The journal has been published since 1997 and often features articles by Rao himself as well as other teachers on the faculty.

Rao's passion can also be understood from the fact that when a court case was filed against astrology, he was the only astrologer who turned up to defend it.[10] The case was initially filed in the High Courts of Andhra Pradesh and Tamil Nadu against India's University Grants Commission (UGC) introducing astrology as a subject in universities in 2000, where the courts ruled in favour of the initiative. Thereafter, the case made its way to the Supreme Court of India in New Delhi and it was here that Rao was admitted as a private petitioner. While many astrologers had previously expressed a willingness to show up, no one eventually did. The case underwent hearings for three years until May 2004 when the presiding judge, Justice G.P. Mathur, upheld the previous judgement as 'astrology is partly based upon study of movement of Sun, Earth, planets, and other celestial bodies, [and so], it is a study of science atleast to some extent'.[11] Of the forty-one universities that had applied for the licence to teach courses in 'Jyotir Vigyan' (the science of Jyotish), only twenty of them were recommended for the final go-ahead.

Today, Bhartiya Vidya Bhavan's course in astrology is one of the most sought-after in India. The teachers, most of them postgraduates, come from varied educational backgrounds such as literature, mathematics, engineering, economics, science, law, and more. The department hosts regular seminars, guest speakers, and follows strict discipline to the point that an irregular or a non-performing student can even be disqualified from the course. Teachers who fail to produce original research too are asked to leave, much like Western academia's 'publish or perish' principle.

Writing in the Silver Jubilee edition of the *Journal of Astrology* in 2012, K.N. Rao expressed satisfaction and pride at the institute's modern and scientific research-oriented approach towards astrology but also rued astrology's image problem. He wrote, 'At the end of my life's journey and mission, I have a desperate feeling that Jyotisha, among intellectual disciplines will always appear rather barbaric, lacking in finesse and civilised breadth because its practitioners appearing in television channels, practising it in streets all over India are poorly educated, avaricious and mistake antiquated approach to be appealing and proper.' He, however, reiterated the distinctiveness of the approach spearheaded by him and was loathe to be put in the same category as the 'old guard emphasising remedies'.

But while traditional astrology had its journey of revival both in India and the US, popular astrology had a new chapter to go through—the commodification of astrology, aided by the internet for the most part.

Notes

1   Robert Schmidt, 'Problem of Astrology' (International Astrology Research Centre, 2000), http://cura.free.fr/decem/09schmi2.html.

2   Chris Brennan, *Robert Zoller: Pioneer in Reviving Medieval Astrology* (The Astrology Podcast, 2020), https://www.youtube.com/watch?v=E5a4Y1U9IW8.

3   Garry Philipson, *An Interview with Robert Zoller* (Skyscript, 2006), https://www.skyscript.co.uk/zoller.html.

4   Garry Phillipson, *An Interview with Robert Hand*, https://www.skyscript.co.uk/rhand.html.

5   Maalok, *Interview with K.N. Rao* (Light on Vedic Astrology reprint, 2020), https://www.lightonvedicastrology.com/blog/interview-with-k-n-rao-conversations-with-an-eminent-vedic-astrologer.

6   K.N. Rao, *Twenty Five Years: Agonies and Ecstasies* (Silver Jubilee Magazine, Institute of Astrology at Bharatiya Vidya Bhavan), p. 30.

7   Ibid., p. 57.

8   K.N. Rao Interview: *Value of Research* (Light on Vedic Astrologyreprint,2020),https://www.lightonvedicastrology.com/blog/k-n-rao-interview-the-value-of-research.

9   Ibid.

10 Maalok, *Interview with K.N. Rao* (Light on Vedic Astrology reprint, 2020), https://www.lightonvedicastrology.com/blog/interview-with-k-n-rao-conversations-with-an-eminent-vedic-astrologer.

11 'P.M. Bhargava & Ors vs University Grants Commission &... on 5 May, 2004', https://indiankanoon.org/doc/697794/

13

Big Astro: *Walter Mercado, Bejan Daruwalla and the Internet*

'You're bigger than Jesus Christ, aren't you?' is what the American radio show host Howard Stern asked the first-ever celebrity astrologer, Walter Mercado, when he came on his show in October 1997. Born to Spanish immigrants in the Ponce village of Puerto Rico in 1932, his spiritual gifts had already been recognised in his childhood. After a neighbour saw him pick up and nurse a dying bird to health, the people in the village became convinced that he was a divine healer and would line up outside his house to touch and kiss his hand. For them, he was the Walter of Miracles. Even as a child, he was fascinated by spirituality of all sorts, including astrology. However, as he grew up, he went to live in the capital city of San Juan, where the theatre and arts scene was exploding and was the perfect fit for a natural performer like Mercado. There he found work with telenovelas and was well-known as an actor in the 1960s.

But the stars realigned his life back with his true destiny. He was asked to fill in for a guest artist at a TV show for a fifteen-minute segment. Dressed up in a dazzling costume and wearing make-up, he talked about astrology with his usual performative flair. It was an immediate hit and the TV network awarded him a regular feature right away. He would show up on TV wearing enchanting capes and a decorated face to give out astrological readings for the twelve zodiac signs. Within three months, he had a one-hour show known as *Walter, Las Estrellas y Usted* (Walter, the Stars and You) in 1969. He would discuss each of the signs and talk about astrological concepts such as the return of Saturn, and other such topics. What made Mercado an enduring hit was the positivism in his readings, signing off from his shows blowing kisses in the air, saying *'Mucho mucho amor'* (much love), which became the title of the Netflix original documentary on his life, *Mucho Mucho Amor: The Legend of Walter Mercado* in 2020.

'He's literally sending out positive vibes at you, one astrological sign at a time,' was how the *Hamilton* actor Lin Manuel Miranda, who appeared on the Netflix documentary as one of the astrologer's fans, described his childhood memories of watching his show. Like Mercado,

Miranda is of Puerto Rican descent as well, where the former's legacy remains amongst the most cherished ones for the country. Speaking about these stints in an interview for the documentary, Mercado said, 'When I entered into the world of astrology, it was a boom. It was a boom. Really, a boom.' He thought it was a combination of the right people, the right audience and the right time. The stars had aligned for him a little too literally. At the same time, his popularity helped solidify not only an even greater association of astrology with tropical Sun signs but also astrology-related services such as TV shows, hotlines, and more.

Then his manager Bill Bakula took him to superstardom. He booked Mercado the first show in history that was entirely dedicated to astrology, with high production quality to boot. In Mercado's words, he made him the prophet of the New Age. This one hour show's segments were broadcast across countries in Europe and the US both on TV and on radio. At one point, over 150 radio channels would play out his readings and close to 120 million people would tune in to listen to him. He landed a book deal with Time Warner, met ambassadors and heads of state from many countries, including the US presidents Bill Clinton and Ronald Reagan. Luxury brands like Versace, Isaac Mizrahi and Swarovski would design his capes for him. With popularity came criticism. In Mercado's case, it was mostly directed towards his androgynous looks, and rumours around his sexuality were rife. But despite that, he thrived in the overwhelmingly Catholic and orthodox Hispanic communities as he was also a source of warmth and emotional support, especially for immigrants living away from home.

At the height of his popularity in 1995, however, Bakula took everything from him. He got Mercado, who considered Bakula his son, to sign an agreement in which the astrologer signed away his brand and everything he had ever created, such as television shows, home tapes, video discs, print material, magazine articles, cable transmission, and more. The time duration of this legal obligation was 'forever' and its territory was the 'Universe'. What followed was a six-year-long court battle where Bakula claimed close to US$ 15 million in damages. Ultimately, the court ruled in favour of Mercado. The last of his astrological reading episodes aired in 2006 and his repeated attempts at making a comeback after that were unsuccessful.

In 2019, HistoryMiami Museum celebrated fifty years of Walter Mercado, displaying his capes and other artefacts, and it immediately brought him back into the limelight. This time, it was the astrology-loving millennials as well as the LGBT communities. He was interviewed by the prominent journalist Jorge Ramos following this, where Mercado discussed his belief in a transcendental consciousness, reincarnation and the soul. He passed away a couple of months later.

While many believe Mercado's legacy is limited to the West, it was perhaps the impetus for astrology-related shows in India and around the world as well. After the introduction of corporate television networks in the early 90s, most news and religion-related channels would have a segment to discuss astrological readings for the week. While most of these channels featured saffron robe-wearing Hindu priests as astrologers, there was one who stood out. It was the affable Bejan Daruwalla.

The Parsi Devotee of Ganesha

Born in 1931 in Gujarat's Bharuch, his family was amongst the richest in the country. As per his own claims, Daruwalla's father was the highest paid merchant–weaver in the history of the country. His relationship with his father was challenging, where the latter often had him against the ropes, especially when it came to astrology. In a BBC interview with the noted Indian journalist Karan Thapar, he recounted the time he was living abroad and received a telegram that said that his father had suffered a heart attack and was on the verge of death. When the son rushed back home, he found his father digging into chicken wings. Daruwalla said he called him 'dumbo' and asked how it was that his astrological knowledge did not tell him that he was, in fact, not dying.

While his family was of Parsi faith (Indian adherents of Zoroastrianism), Daruwalla was an ardent devotee of the Hindu God Lord Ganesha, who is the patron deity of Jyotish, among other things. He never spoke without offering his salutations to him first and would even compare his own potbelly with that of the elephant God.[1] A story he often liked to narrate was that he found his flair for prophecy and showmanship at the age of five when some older schoolgirls came to him and asked him if they would clear their school exams. He told some of them that they would, others wouldn't, and for still others he recited a gibberish incantation. But he was surprised that they believed him and took his word for it.[2]

He went on to study English at college and taught as a professor before venturing into astrology. As an astrologer, Daruwalla would consult for many prominent Indian figures such as industrialist Dhirubai Ambani, former home minister, Sushil Kumar Shinde, Indian classical music maestro Pandit Jasraj, and more. He claimed to have read for the current Indian Prime Minister Narendra Modi as well, which landed the latter in a controversy amongst his political rivals. Unlike most full-time astrologers of his time, he could converse in both English and Hindi and that made him a go-to candidate whenever news channels wanted an astrologer to weigh in on a significant news cycle. He would often appear on prominent English-language news channels such as NDTV, CNBC, and others to give his astrological take on latest issues.

But what made him likeable was that he was quick to laugh at himself and had a lot of natural charm, which is something one doesn't expect from most Indian astrologers even today. In 1978, he accompanied the film crew of the Bollywood movie *Ahinsa*, starring superstars Sunil Dutt and Rekha, when they were shooting the last scene of the movie. The scene involved horses galloping away against the backdrop of a setting Sun, but at the time of shooting, the horses refused to move. When Daruwalla was asked if they would move, he said they would, but in five minutes. The horses did kick off just then and people asked him how he was able to predict that. In his characteristically self-deprecating manner, he responded, 'One donkey knows another donkey.'[3] A couple of decades later, he appeared on Shekhar Suman's late-night talk show, *Movers and Shakers*, along with Bollywood actress Bipasha Basu. On the show, he poked fun at the inappropriateness of him being an astrologer as a Daruwalla (literally, someone who sold alcohol), read Suman's and Basu's hands, and promoted his English language annual horoscope books. These books, the first of their kind, were often sold at gift shops. They were the size of pocketbooks and included predictions for career, relationships and personal growth for all zodiac signs. Till date, Daruwalla's books remain the only such astrological books for English-literate enthusiasts in India.

When it came to astrology, he took a measured approach. Having married and separated twice, he said he took his own birth chart with not just a 'pinch of salt but a bucketful of salt'. While he had been able to predict the death of former Indian Prime Minister Indira Gandhi as well as the violent and untimely death of her heir-apparent, Sanjay Gandhi, he entreated astrologers to be more tolerant. He wanted them to understand that each individual is unique, and so even if astrology relies on patterns, it might not apply in the same way for everyone. The tolerance of that difference was what distinguished a good astrologer from a bad one for Daruwalla.[4] He worked right till the end of his days, until the ripe old age of eighty-eight. His annual horoscopes shifted from print to YouTube videos and after his passing in 2020, the mantle has been taken up by his son, Nastur Daruwalla.

Today, Indian TV channels regularly feature astrology-related shows that have an astrologer give out weekly predictions for all zodiac signs. These channels are in various Indian languages and are broadcast not just in the country but across the world, owing to a global Indian diaspora. Lawmakers and policymakers have often tried to bring a stop to astrology programmes, but without success. In 2013, the Ministry of Information and Broadcasting issued a strict advisory against broadcast of shows and advertorials 'which appear to encourage superstition and blind belief'.[5] It had the unanimous support of thinkers of all stripes, going beyond political partisanship. Even astrologer Niranjan Babu, B.V. Raman's son, extended support 'as long as restrictions [were] not extended to the practice of astrology'. He believed that astrologers that dress up for the part and give out sensationalistic predictions create fear amongst the general populace and are not good for the society.[6] However, the courts refused to prohibit these shows as 'they [were] not in violation of the Programme Code and the Advertising Code' as per Indian law.[7] Today, such shows and ads continue unabated, reaching millions of Indian viewers daily. Many astrologers even seek to up their offline business by marketing how many shows they appear on. Their rivals, to undercut their influence, can resort to huge billboards to stand out. All in all, at least since late 90s, it has been practically impossible to live in India and not have astrology business in one's face in one form or the other.

Astrology.com

Astrology took off across the world when the internet and information technology came into play. Unlike his counterpart from the 1970s and before, the modern astrologer could now leave much of the traditional work of charting out a birth chart to the computer. Where earlier one had to have a good grasp of astronomy and mathematics in order to draw up a chart, one didn't need those skills anymore to be an astrologer. Of course, this meant that pretty much anyone could jump on the astrology bandwagon—as long as they were perceptive enough to gauge a client's situation and use a little bit of common sense along with basic astrological knowledge in delivering a commercial reading.

Most astrology softwares, websites and apps today make use of Swiss Ephemeris developed by NASA's Jet Propulsion Laboratory. Amongst serious professionals, Sirius is still the most popular software when it comes to Western astrologers. It was developed by an American company in 2008 and costs over US$ 500. But it does a lot more at the click of a mouse than astrologers of antiquity could ever have imagined possible. To start with, it can list the position of, say Mars or a particular star in the Orion constellation, at any point of time from 5400 BCE to 5400 CE. Or it can show you information about how the night sky looks in over 260,000 cities across the world at the moment. Various astrological texts and principles are coded into the software and so the same birth chart could be read from any of the Hellenistic, Hindu or even psychological astrological perspectives. The software can readily chart out details about an individual's career, relationship and financial issues, as well as how latest transits may affect them. This leaves the modern astrologer to do only the job of interpretation.

Jagannath Hora and Parashara's Light, on the other hand, are preferred by Jyotishis or Vedic astrologers. Of these, the former was developed in 2003 by engineer and astrologer P.V.R. Narasimha Rao. It is available free of cost and its features, in addition to the ones that are found in Sirius, include a variety of panchangs, three hundred different kinds of birth charts, and more. Parashara's Light is a paid software and costs around US $400. What's different with this one is that it includes educational tools such as an astrological dictionary, pre-designed worksheets and digital versions of four classic Jyotish texts.

With this, many astrologers could now set up a website and start offering readings via email. These were either delivered as an audio or a video recording or simply a text-based report. Their market was now the entire world, not just the immediate neighbourhood as before. The astrologer could be sitting in a tier 2 town in India and have clients in Europe, US, China and more. The readings could be about one's career, relationships or simply something about finding one's true purpose in life, and cost anything upwards of US$ 100.

But even if one could not navigate their way around a software or didn't feel comfortable spending any money on a reading, one could always log on to an astrology website. In fact, even before astrology softwares showed up on the scene, there was the Switzerland-based Astrodienst.[8] It was started in 1980 by Alois Trendl, who had begun studying astrology as an amateur a year before. He had stumbled upon a book on how to draw up one's birth chart, but when he asked his mother for the time of his birth, she did not know the correct time. So, he accessed his medical records and found himself to be a Taurus rising, which resonated with him. Having studied computer science for almost a decade by that point, he decided to write a software to create birth charts. His girlfriend at the time was a psychotherapist who collected the birth-data of some sixty-odd clients, and so the couple began studying their charts for psychological insights into them. Eventually, Trendl was convinced there was something to astrology and kept exploring it while also pursuing his PhD.

In 1981, Trendl contacted astrology schools in Germany to help design his charts. He also got in touch with Liz Greene, who took a psychological approach to reading a chart, and by 1987, the duo launched Psychological Horoscope Analysis. This was before the age of the internet, and the horoscopes were sent by mail. Despite that, the response was overwhelmingly positive and at this point, the company was licensing the software in over twenty countries around the world. When the internet came around, the website was launched in 1996. The Psychological Horoscope Analysis could now be accessed online for US$ 65 in many languages including Chinese, Portuguese, Russian, and more. In its current form, it is an 18-25 page report that looks at an individual's psychological type, character and shadow traits, the impact of family background on one's psyche, one's relationship patterns and the potential for psychological growth in life. This report, in addition to free chart-drawing and an Astro Databank where one can access birth-timings of famous personalities for research, has cemented Astrodienst's place as the top resource for astrology enthusiasts worldwide. Today, more users access the website on their smartphones than on the desktop.

India's AstroSage, which exclusively uses Jyotish, is another favourite with enthusiasts and professionals alike. Launched in 2008 by the Uttar Pradesh-based brothers, Puneet Pandey and Pratik Pandey, it is now available both as a website and as an app. Its free birth chart reading includes the chart, its interpretation, the dashas or time periods in one's life and remedies one can perform, among other features. It also allows users to match horoscopes for a couple for free and if one needs a consultation, one can quickly get in touch with an astrologer over call for a nominal price.

Both of these websites receive heavy traffic and consistently top the ranking board for astrology and spirituality-related domains. There are now countless such websites with similar features, catering to enthusiasts of different astrological systems. For the first time in the history of astrology, anyone can now draw a chart and find at least a rudimentary interpretation for it. All of this is online, free, and doesn't take more than five minutes. It also doesn't require one to sacrifice one's privacy to an astrologer. This was not possible a mere four decades ago when one had to get in touch with an astrologer to get a chart drawn and understand its meaning. So, while most people today at least know their Sun sign according to tropical astrology, the enthusiasts will generally know their astrological placements in sufficient detail and will have had at least one consultation via phone, email or Skype.

This increasing awareness led to two forms of commercialisation. For the pop astrology lovers, there was a plethora of zodiac-themed products to choose from. A Cancerian could now buy a plush pillow that had the crab symbol over it to feel more at home, which is just what you would expect a Cancerian to do. Or a Sagittarius could rock a bow pendant because everyone must know who they were dealing with right off the bat. Merchandise of all sorts—clothing, personal accessories, showpieces—have flooded the consumerist economies since the early 2000s.

At the same time, with the easy accessibility of astrological readings, whether free or paid, there has been a constant risk of obfuscation, much like Leo's overly simplified delineations in the early twentieth century. This can be particularly concerning considering anyone can claim to be an astrologer and disseminate potentially harmful information. To date, there is no regulating authority or self-correcting mechanism that can keep this in check. However, this hasn't stopped astrology from growing. In the post 2008 economic recession era, social media and apps have led to a new wave of astrology.

Notes

1   Pankaj Pachauri, *Money Mantra with Bejan Daruwalla* (NDTV Profit), https://www.youtube.com/watch?v=mj5d98L0 Yu4.

2   Shekhar Suman, *Movers and Shakers* Episode 35 (Sony Entertainment Television, 1998), https://www.youtube.com/watch?v=zetzJHzEWAQ.

3   Karan Thapar, *Interview with Bejan Daruwalla* (BBC, 1999), https://www.youtube.com/watch?v=LwWdNScsdt0.

4   Ibid.

5   Ministry of Information and Broadcasting, Advisory (Government of India, 2013), https://docs.google.com/file/d/0B4ADrfUIhVGtdzRfYXF4N1d2bWM/view?resourcekey=0-V_Rcx6iHNmasAjeZbG8WVg.

6   M.A. Kanathanda, 'Future Bleak for Astrology Shows on TV' (*Times of India*, 10 December 2015), https://timesofindia.indiatimes.com/city/bengaluru/Future-bleak-for-astrology-shows-on-TV/articleshow/50115828.cms.

7   'Court Refuses to Ban Astrology-based TV shows' (*The Hindu*, 14 December 2014), https://www.thehindu.com/news/national/court-refuses-to-ban-astrologybased-tv-shows/article6690738.ece.

8   Chris Brennan, Alois Treindl Interview: *The Founder of Astrodienst* (The Astrology Podcast, 2018), https://www.youtube.com/watch?v=ziGo31gZAjo.

14

Astrology as Counterculture:
The American Millennial and New Spirituality

It says something about human nature and its intrinsic affinity towards astrology that its most potent boom came in the twenty-first century. It's potent not because there are believers but because there are believers despite the realities of the International Space Station and the Hubble telescope. We actually don't need our cosmologies anymore or anything that came of it and yet, here we are.

It befuddles many, but not Chris Brennan. He found astrology as a teenager at the turn of the twenty-first century. Born in 1984 in the US, he picked up a book about the famous French astrologer Nostradamus and was immediately intrigued. Later, he found the website Astrodienst where he could look up not just his but anyone's birth chart for free. With this, he was hooked. So, when the time came to attend university after graduating high school, he chose to study astrology at Kepler College in Seattle. He was especially looking forward to studying psychological astrology, but the stars had other plans for him.

Launched in 2000, the college is named after astronomer Johannes Kepler, given his abiding love for astrology. Brennan attended the institute between 2003 and 2006, where he studied traditional astrology systems and specialised in Hellenistic astrology because the psychological track was not available yet. He graduated with an Associate of Arts degree in astrological studies and worked with Project Hindsight for a couple of years. Eventually, he launched his own practice as an astrologer and worked on several projects to increase awareness about astrology. One of these was working as an editor for astrology articles on Wikipedia. He had to leave that soon enough though, because the sceptical editors far outnumbered the astrologer editors, both in number and influence.

In 2010, he heard that degree programmes in his alma mater were being shut down. This included the degree he had earned as well as the bachelor's and master's in Eastern and Western Traditions: The History, Philosophy, and Transmission of Astrology. This was a direct result of academics and experts from other fields pressurising the region's higher education body to put an end to any programme associated with astrology. John Silber, former chancellor at Boston University, felt that the college was '[honouring] Kepler not for his strength but for his weakness, as if a society advocating drunkenness named a school for Ernest Hemingway'.[1] Since then, the college has only been able to offer online certifications.

While Brennan was disappointed to hear the news, he felt that the college had still managed to raise the standard of serious astrological study even in its short tenure. Speaking at Kepler College's final graduation ceremony, he emphasised, 'Kepler graduates are unique because they have not just been exposed to every major tradition of astrology, but they are actually fully conversant in all of the different traditions. And this is not just limited to their knowledge of practical techniques, but they are also familiar with the history and the philosophy of the different traditions as well. They know where the different schools of astrology came from, how they were developed and transmitted, and how astrologers in different eras conceptualised astrology and integrated into their worldview.'[2]

He would later use this openness to exploring astrology in all its shapes and forms to set up his widely popular *The Astrology Podcast* in 2012. Brennan also started posting videos to YouTube and encouraged by the response, signed up for Patreon in 2015. The platform lets audience members who pay for content created by content creators across varying mediums and professions become patrons. In his promotional video for the podcast, Brennan likened himself to a man named Cyrus who was a patron for Ptolemy and to whom the latter dedicated his *Tetrabiblos*. Today, the podcast has over fourteen hundred patrons who pay anything between one and twenty-five dollars per episode. This money helps Brennan produce high-quality podcast content for his audience.

With over three hundred episodes in his archive already, Brennan releases an average of four to six episodes every month. These episodes are usually one to two hours long and feature discussions with astrologers, academics and sometimes, even non-astrologers. The Astrology Podcast is one of the most important platforms in the world for intellectually critical discourse on the history, philosophy and transmission of astrology today. Most of his podcasts are also available on his YouTube channel, which boasts of thousands of subscribers. He also offers about fifteen different courses in astrology online, including one on Hellenistic Astrology and another on how to become a successful professional astrologer. The latter course includes topics such as researching one's market, establishing appropriate expectations with clients, selecting auspicious dates for consultations and legality of astrology in one's area, ethics, client confidentiality, and dealing with difficult clients, among others.

Millennials in the West form a huge chunk of his audience, and so Brennan's podcast often reflects how they experience astrology. For instance, he has episodes where his guests speak about Mercury Retrogrades and Saturn Returns. The former is a fairly regular event during the year and can cause mishaps in communication and travel. The latter, on the other hand, is the return of Saturn to one's natal Saturn sign which happens between the ages of twenty-seven and thirty for everyone. While the former can cause temporary setbacks, the latter is a rite of passage through which one formally enters adulthood and experiences major life changes.

Of Mercury Retrogrades and Saturn Returns

Mercury Retrograde is not only the source of many astrological memes but is used even by companies to sell products. These include Huda Beauty's US$ 67 Mercury Retrograde eyeshadow palette and numerous generic products rebranded by lifestyle magazines like Elle and Vogue as helping 'to get you through' the unsettling transit.

Saturn Returns, however, tend not to be diluted in this way. Instead, popular astrologers often specialise in guiding millennials through their Saturn Returns, often the first major upheaval in life for many. This can include moving into a new home, changing careers, getting married or even shifting to a new country. When Discovery's TLC launched an astrology-focused show, *Stargazing*, in December 2018, the first episode discussed Saturn Returns in detail. The episode dove into the lessons of the transit—live authentically, be willing to change and be mindful of future goals. An astrologer did an in-person reading and explored Saturn Returns of celebrities. J.K. Rowling is said to have published the first Harry Potter book during hers, while Beyonce released her hit single,

Run The World, and had a baby during her Saturn Return.

Stargazing had a total of ten episodes, each around ten minutes long. Discussing some popular astrological themes, its two hosts '[revealed] these concepts through a pop culture lens, relating the cosmos to hair and makeup look, style and interior décor trends, astro-themed goods (jewellery, stones, candles), aura photography, and more.'[3]

But why would a major American network commission a show on astrology? Well—because it's cool now. This may be, in part, due to the Co-Star App, which caught on with millennials because of its irreverent one-liner astrological forecasts that show up as push notifications on your phone. Titled 'Your Day at a Glance', the alerts say things like 'avoiding your ex's social media is always a good idea' or 'falling out of touch with reality is the same as using drugs to escape it', or quite simply, 'check your ego'. The punchiness of these appeal to social media-savvy millennials, who often share them on Twitter or Instagram, just for fun.

Co-Star was launched in October 2017 by Banu Guler during her own Saturn Return. Born in Texas to Pakistani and Turkish parents, she grew up around astrology, palmistry and numerology. Speaking to Brennan for his podcast, she recounted how she first worked as a bike messenger and then as a graphic artist for the fashion brand Michael Kors when she got the idea for the app.[4] Some of the app's initial users were staff from her workplace, and their encouragement pushed Guler to take it to the next level. While the American spirituality and astrology market is pegged at US$ 2 billion,[5] this app alone has managed to raise US$ 6 million from seed investors so far. By 2020, the app already had more than seven million registered users. Of the 195 countries in the world, Co-Star is active in 192.

In Co-Star's universe, astrology is in some ways more than, well, astrology. The app considers itself 'a catalyst for collectivity in a chaotic world: to see and be seen frees us to find our place in the universe'. It seeks to help you connect more meaningfully with people in your life, tread carefully with strangers and what and whom to pay attention to in a sea of small talk. Along with the push notifications and hyper-personalised free birth chart interpretations, Co-Star has also curated its social media in a way that is designed to hook the millennial astrology enthusiast. A post could talk about social faux pas common to each sign—the Aries individual would have disruptive side conversations during work meetings, the Virgo would consider her constructive criticism as a love language and an Aquarius would be the sort to preface lukewarm opinions with 'hot takes'. Its Instagram account is followed by almost two million users.

Applying Astrology

Following Co-Star's lead, similar astrology apps that focus on millennials have cropped up in recent years. One of these is the Los Angeles-based Struck. At present, it is available only in select cities such as New York City, Chicago and the Bay Area in San Francisco, with plans to expand further. Launched in late 2019 by Rachel Lo, the daughter of immigrants from Hong Kong, Struck is a matchmaking and dating app. A user is matched to profiles that are compatible with them astrologically. While swiping on Tinder made dating seem mechanical to Lo, Struck uses astrology to make it enjoyable and 'inspire meaningful coincidences'. For this, the app looks at two hundred different aspects in a birth chart to understand the synastry, or compatibility, between two individuals. Because it is marketed as a matchmaking app, it also received attention due to an unexpected reason— the Netflix show *Indian Matchmaking* which explores arranged marriages amongst Indian communities was released around the same time as the app. Ironically, it is in the landscape of arranged marriages that matching of horoscopes plays a crucial role in deciding whether two families should go ahead with a marriage. Choosing a serious relationship or a life partner clearly remains a gamble for many and they find it useful to seek astrological guidance, whether they live in the posh Upper East Side of Manhattan or belong to a tier 2 town in India's Rajasthan.

But that's not all. Even Tinder has taken note and upped its game. The app now allows users to add astrological markers to their profiles and the website version has a blog dedicated to astrology. In one of the articles, for instance, one can learn how to write an accurate bio according to one's zodiac sign.

Snapchat, now Snap, is another popular social networking app that has added astrology to its features. A user can now add their astrological profile to their handle, and it lists twelve placements—the zodiac signs in which a user has their Sun, Moon, ascendant or rising, and the nine planets. Snap also lets you calculate your compatibility with another user, which is ironically a feature missing from Tinder.

With all of this, could TikTok be far behind? The Chinese app that made waves across the world in 2019, rivalling Instagram in popularity, features astrological accounts too. The most famous of these is that of Maren Altman, a New York University philosophy graduate. She graduated just before the pandemic and found herself without a job. That's when Altman, born in 1998, set up her TikTok account, with her first video talking about how Scorpio and Gemini people act when in love. It blew up, which can be a precursor to social media fame, and then, finding herself with all the time in the world, Altman began putting out even more astrology-related content. Her videos were short and snappy, with an astrological chart beaming in the background as Altman spoke in her signature tongue-in-cheek manner. Altman, who had been into astrology since high school where she would charge US$ 30 for thirty-minute readings at parties, has now converted her Manhattan apartment into her studio.

Altman prefers financial astrology over Sun sign astrology and feels comparing the two is like 'comparing Fisher-Price to a Tesla, not that one is better or worse'.[6] On her podcast, *Modern Magic*, she discusses topics like the astrology of bitcoin. The cryptocurrency bitcoin is studied with its 'birth' details as 3 January 2009, at 1.15 p.m. in New York, the day it was first released on an open-source software. In the summer of 2020, Altman launched her online school called Astrology Academy. Anyone can join this school for either twelve monthly payments of US$ 139 or a one-time payment of US$ 1,499. After signing up, a user can avail of her astrological library which has hours of self-paced lectures, weekly interactions with Altman and access to her private Facebook community.

Like her, the popular Twitter handle Astro Poets also managed to get something concrete out of making astrology-related social media posts—a book deal. Published by Macmillan's Flatiron Books in late 2019, the Astro Poets book is an extension of their viral tweets which can best be described as sassy poetry. They mimic the Linda Goodman template which has been reimagined for the modern millennial. So now one can know what it's like to date, befriend and text a particular zodiac sign. Queer communities also form a substantial part of their readership. Alex Dimitrov, one of the two poets behind the brand, explained in an interview that 'to be queer is to live in a space that's in flux, and poetry and astrology also live in that space'.[7]

Books, Series and Beyond

In the current century, astrology is not a weird relic of the past. It is, in fact, woke—having extended the astrological paradigm to include the otherwise under-represented sexual and racial minorities in the West. Colin Bedell, a gay astrologer based in New York, describes himself as a 'queer Gemini Twin' and has written three books on astrology—most notably, *Queer Cosmos: The Astrology of Queer Identities and Relationships*, published by Simon and

Schuster in 2019. He has also written columns regularly for lifestyle and wellness magazines like *Cosmopolitan* and *Well+Good*, where he looks at the latest prominent headlines from an astrological perspective. For one of his columns, for instance, Bedell looked at the astrological compatibility of Kamala Harris and Joe Biden, the Democrat duo elected to lead the US government in 2021. The partnership, he wrote, showed 'compelling potential' as their astrological polarity would give them an 'opportunity to move beyond dilemma and paradox into a place of unity and win/win situations for all parties'.[8] Other such popular columns include *New York Magazine's* 'Madame Clairevoyant', which is the pseudonym of the US-based fiction writer Claire Comstock-Gay and Alice Sparkly Kat's work published on her own website. Kat is also the author of *Postcolonial Astrology: Reading the Planets through Capital, Power, and Labor*, which was published by Penguin Random House in 2021. These writers offer a perspective on the socio-political issues of the day in a way that is unlike traditional astrology and is heavily influenced by progressive ideas that are not found in astrological texts and works of pre-modern astrologers.

Another US-based astrologer, Chani Nicholas, wrote a book titled *You Were Born for This: Astrology for Radical Self-Acceptance*. Published by HarperOne in 2020, it featured themes of progressive politics and queer identity. The book received glowing reviews from *The New York Times*, *Vanity Fair*, *Oprah Magazine*, *Los Angeles Times*, and more. The same year, she launched her own astrology app too. The Chani App, as it is called, is 'astrology for self-discovery, mindfulness, and healing'. Nicholas also featured on a promotional series for Netflix where she read the birth chart of the Hollywood actress Jane Fonda.

It was around this time that Netflix aired two astrology-related offerings—*Mucho Mucho Amor: The Legend of Walter Mercado* and BBC's *The Luminaries*. The latter was a cinematic adaption of the 2013 Man Booker Prize-winning novel of the same name by the New Zealand author, Eleanor Catton. It is, to date, one of the very few highly acclaimed works in literature and television that feature astrological motifs as a prominent story arc. The novel follows mysterious events that take place during the gold rush in nineteenth-century New Zealand, with astrological indications giving a foreboding of what is to come in a particular chapter. It exhibits at least a working knowledge of astrology, and Catton has remarked in an interview that 'someone said I must have been an Indian in my past life because I've written a book about gold and astrology'.[9]

Astrology and Glamour

In the age of capitalism, astrology is glamourous and luxe too. There have been high-end zodiac-themed products such as Prada's Cahier Astrology bag ($2,090) and Emilio Pucci's Zodiac boots ($5575) on the market. On the American e-commerce platform, Etsy, one can buy vintage astrological products such as old horoscopes, works of art and other miscellaneous products such as a constellation-themed 1990 Robert Cavalli denim jacket worth US$ 550.

The entertainment industry Goddesses swear by astrology too. At least three of the most popular singers in the West—Madonna, Taylor Swift and Adele—seem to believe in it. French DJ David Guetta revealed in an interview that in 2011, Madonna, a Leo, refused to work with Guetta, a Scorpio, as the two signs were incompatible, liable to butt heads, and be confrontational with each other.[10] Taylor Swift, a Sagittarius, believes she owes her blind optimism, love for travel and adventure, and independence to her Sun sign.[11] Adele, in a tell-all interview after a long absence from public life, spoke about how she went through a divorce during her Saturn Return. She said that she 'lost the plot' during this time of her life and that her Saturn Return forced her to question her identity, priorities and happiness.[12] Popular English actress Helena Bonham Carter consulted an astrologer friend to research for her role as Princess Margaret for the Netflix series *The Crown*. Her friend, Carter revealed in an interview, could give her insights into the Leo princess more quickly than anyone else.[13] It is worth recalling that it was because of the princess that we have newspaper horoscopes and zodiacal stereotypes in the first place. It was on her birth that R.H. Naylor first published her horoscope in Britain, which later developed into a daily horoscope for all signs.

The Modern Critique of Astrology

The media has been tracking the rising popularity of astrology in the West. In 2018, *The Guardian* asked why millennials were into astrology[14] and the next year, *The New Yorker* wrote about how millennials were driving the revival of astrology as a consequence of living 'in the age of uncertainty'.[15] That same year, *The New York Times* reported on venture capital funding in 'Big Zodiac' and why it seemed pre-ordained. Astrology, according to the article, was having a 'cultural moment' because people needed to feel a sense of community in the face of the decline of organised religion. Millennials, it turned out, weren't getting enough of a dopamine fix from their social media followers. Personalising the narrative of their lives felt good to them, which is where astrology came in.[16]

But not everyone is buying into the madness. When Susan Miller, considered a successor to Linda Goodman, said that 2020 was going to be a great and prosperous year, people believed her. Miller is best known for her lengthy monthly horoscopes for each zodiac sign, which she has been publishing for over two decades. Astrology enthusiasts swear by her forecasts but were left severely disappointed in the year of Covid-19. Some criticised her on social media, asking why she couldn't predict what was going to happen. To pacify her audience, she put out 'The 2020 Coronavirus Outlook' in mid-March. Comparing the charts of 2020 and 1918, the year of the Spanish Flu, Miller wrote that Pluto and Jupiter orbiting together tightly was the reason for these pandemics. Goading the reader to 'have faith', she claimed both that the virus would be over quickly and that it would take time to leave, which was a tad oversmart, perhaps. The prognosis, published on her website, has now been removed.

Quartz, the digital media publication, felt that the problem with modern astrology was not one of astrology but psychology. It took issue with how 'even if an astrological configuration spells trouble, the modern astrologer will describe it as an "opportunity for growth", as if they were a patronising middle-manager'. It eschewed the 'mushy hocus-pocus' of the psychological brand of astrology as it 'accentuates internal matters of the mind and spirit, [opening] up far too much room for confirmation bias'. Instead, it pointed out that the story of revival of ancient astrological texts was what the modern astrologer needed to watch out for.[17] This sentiment was echoed by *The Guardian*, where the writer wrote about the usefulness of a 'true astrological revival' because astrology could 'bring a long-term perspective to changes, rather than keeping them in a sometimes terrifying present'.[18]

In January 2020, data analyst Alexander Boxer combined his penchant for data with astrology and published his book, *A Scheme of Heaven: The History of Astrology and the Search for Our Destiny in Data*. The book traced the history of astrology and astronomy from Babylonia to the landing of the lunar aircraft Apollo 11. Boxer pointed out that it was astrological thought that influenced important astronomical discoveries, and that despite astrology's various ups and downs, it has managed to stay surprisingly resilient. He also made a provocative assertion—astrology was just as algorithmic as artificial intelligence (AI). He explained in an interview, 'Astrology was an expression of a deeply mathematically deterministic view of the human condition. That seems to be the direction many of our current technologies are heading in—the idea that we can be described pretty well with certain fairly simple algorithms that predict what you're going to buy, how you're going to vote, where you're going to go, when you're likely to keel over and die.'[19]

Challenges for the Future

Astrology in the modern West, then, is not a mere fringe community. While the astrologer of yore was seen as a learned individual or a sage, astrologers today can be professionals working in medicine, finance or the performing arts. They might pursue astrology out of passion and might not even charge for any service they may provide. Then there are those like Brennan who make their living out of astrology. Their challenges, unlike their ancient counterparts, are manifold.

The first challenge is that of the legitimacy of their chosen field and practice. The dawn of the Enlightenment era in the Western world saw astrology fall from its pedestal down into the gutters. Where earlier it was seen as the mother of astronomy and performed an important religious function for most of human history, now it was a discarded piece of trash. While it never completely disappeared and many great minds dabbled in it time and again, astrology has struggled to regain its past glory. It continues to be seen as a pseudoscience and hence taboo by educated society, particularly in the West, where it was never as ingrained in daily life as it was in India and other Eastern societies.

Professional and full-time astrologers are often at pains to justify their existence to the world. They are constantly trying to explain what astrology is and how or why it works to uninitiated sceptics. But their attempts are greeted with caution at best and outright ridicule at worst. Astrologers today deal with a stigmatisation that would have perplexed their ancient counterparts. To stay relevant, modern astrologers have had to adapt with the times in more ways than one. In the last couple of decades, they have begun to organise themselves like other professionals. But regulating something as ancient, diverse and universal as astrology has proven to be a challenge as well. For one, the multitude of astrological systems and the variety of techniques even within a particular system makes the endeavour fraught with disagreements within the astrological community. It also doesn't help that astrologers often go with what 'works' for them intuitively and through experience, even if it has little to do with what astrological texts dictate.

Be that as it may, the need to professionalise astrology was felt because the work of astrologers is greatly impacted by the laws and policies of the land.[20] Because it is not recognised as a legitimate profession in most countries, astrologers today struggle for basic professional rights. For instance, to register for a business licence in the US, astrologers have to put out a disclaimer that their work is 'for entertainment purposes only', as fortune-telling is punishable by law in the country. This also prevents them from using online payment platforms like Stripe since astrology is not listed as a service or marketing tools like Mailchimp because astrological material is subject to greater scrutiny.

When it comes to imparting astrology education, laws have again posed challenges as seen with the case of Kepler College. So, even though some have attempted classroom-style education, it does not yield the same benefits as, say, an MBA, due to lack of accreditation. Astrologers are further divided amongst themselves on this issue, because while a formal education may help them gain legitimacy and credibility, many still favour the traditional master–student dynamic, even in Western communities. This is because an astrologer's skill depends on personal experience and learning, so studying astrology under an astrologer of repute is believed to be a more credible education.

To address the gamut of concerns that have arisen, astrologers have begun to organise in the past couple of decades. While the American Federation of Astrologers, the first astrology-related organization in the US, was set up in 1938, there has been a greater mobilisation recently. These organisations allow for networking amongst astrologers, conduct conferences, and now even give out certifications. The Northwest Astrological Conference, or NORWAC, is one of the most prominent astrology conferences in the US. It was set up in Seattle in 1984 by Margaret Nalbandian, who founded Kepler College as well. It is a family-run annual conference that sees participation from thousands of astrologers from the country and abroad.

Other such conferences include the United Astrology

Conference that takes place every four to six years and is billed as the 'world's largest gathering of astrologers', with participation from astrologers across the different astrological systems. It has been held since 1995. Brennan says he used to be the youngest person at these conferences for years. In the past three to four years, however, more and more young people are showing up and embracing astrology seriously. In fact, not just the young but the under-represented groups have organised themselves into astrology conferences too. This includes the Queer Astrology Conference. Set up in San Francisco in 2013, it takes place every two years and has featured discussions like Saturn Return of AIDS and how to interact with transgender and non-binary clients.

Brennan, in his almost two decades of working in astrology, makes sure to keep testing his own confirmation biases every now and then. He wants to be certain that he is not wasting his and everyone's time by talking about astrology. However, time and again, he has found his beliefs reaffirmed and the phenomenon of astrology upheld as legitimate. His advice to sceptics is to start by studying their own birth chart and if astrology doesn't work, he says, then nothing in it should ring true.

Clearly Brennan is as much of an entrepreneur as an astrologer who believes in both of his crafts entirely. In his mid-thirties, he lives and breathes astrology. There are many more young astrologers like him in the West today who take astrology extremely seriously and have created a personal brand around themselves through their websites, social media and other online mediums. They have created online communities where they discuss the latest transits, celebrity astrology and astrological thought freely. These astrologers belong to different schools of astrology and are constantly pushing the envelope in using it progressively. They are not the eccentric wizards of the past; they are savvy globetrotters who are one with the times. Whether it's politics or prevailing socio-economic concerns, they are quick to give their astrological take on the latest issues on their social media accounts. For them, in the absence of offline religious and societal communities, such online spaces not only act as professional sounding boards but also help them in building a potential client base.

Enthusiasts often end up finding the likes of Brennan after coming to astrology by way of astrological memes. Social media platforms such as Instagram, Twitter and Facebook are rife with memes that bring out zodiacal stereotypes or the latest transits. Drawing on popular shows, celebrities and self-deprecating humour typical to millennials, these memes can convey the same amount of information as a lengthy Linda Goodman description, but almost instantaneously. While some enthusiasts end up delving deeper into astrology, many only care about finding their rising, Sun and Moon signs to inculcate these in the larger personal narratives of their selves. It is mostly harmless fun but it can also take a negative turn when they end up perpetuating astrological stereotypes in a less savoury way—refusing to date, befriend, live or work with an individual of a particular zodiac sign. Brennan believes it is something professional astrologers should address as much as possible lest it ends up being counterproductive.

It remains to be seen how astrology will shape up in the West in the coming decades, but the way it has been revived, both for the casual and the serious audience, definitely offers food for thought. Whether it's owing to the lack of community life previously granted due to religious gatherings and beliefs or simply a millennial fad, it is unlike anything seen before. Astrology's appeal, then, may have less to do with the stars themselves and more about how they can consistently aid our meaning-making of ourselves and the world around us.

Notes

1   Robert McClure, 'Astrology School Sets Off Controversy' (*Seattle Post-Intelligencer*, 2021), https://www.seattlepi.com/local/article/Astrology-school-sets-off-controversy-1060562.php

2   Kepler College, Chris Brennan 2012 Kepler College Graduation (Kepler College, 2012), https://www.youtube.com/watch?v=sxyYrrYJ1l8

3   'TLC Premiers Latest Digital Original "Stargazing" on Facebook Watch' (*MarketScreener*, 2018), https://m.marketscreener.com/quote/stock/DISCOVERY-INC-9015/news/Discovery-TLC-Premieres-Latest-Digital-Original-ldquo-Stargazing-rdquo-on-Facebook-Watch-27733050/.

4   'Chris Brennan, Co-Star and the Making of a Popular Astrology App' (The Astrology Podcast, 2021), https://www.youtube.com/watch?v=aN0AtSHxN6Q.

5   Erin Griffith, 'Astrology: Venture Capitalists Put Their Money Into the $2.1 Bn Industry' (*The Independent*, 26 April 2019), https://www.independent.co.uk/life-style/horoscopes-

astrology-industry-venture-capitalists-aquarius-a8886341. html

6   Katie Heaney, 'The Most Serious Astrologer on Tiktok' (*The Cut*, 14 January 2021), https://www.thecut.com/2021/01/ maren-altman-viral-tiktok-astrologer.html.

7   Emma Specter, 'Read the Astro Poets' New Astrology Book and It Will Read You' (*Vogue*, 30 October 2019), https:// www.vogue.com/article/astro-poets-book-interview.

8   Colin Bedell, 'Politically Charged: The Astrological Compatibility of Kamala Harris and Joe Biden' (*Well + Good*, 17 August 2020), https://www.wellandgood.com/ astrological-compatibility-harris-biden/.

9   Elizabeth Kuruvilla, feature on Eleanor Catton (*Mint*, 26 January 2015), https://www.livemint.com/Leisure/ pzEq1u3frRLWQehmXjyzHL/Eleanor-Catton-In-the-last-year-Ive-really-struggled-with.html.

10 'Like a Virgo' (*The Guardian*, 5 October 2020), https://www. theguardian.com/news/series/pass-notes/2020/oct/05/all.

11 'Taylor Swift: Part of Me Just Wants to Be Alone' (*Vibe*, 14 January 2013), https://www.vibe.com/news/national/ taylor-swift-part-me-just-wants-be-alone-130116/.

12 Abby Aguirre, 'Adele on the Other Side' (*Vogue*, 7 October 2021), https://www.vogue.com/article/adele-cover-november-2021.

13 Liam Freeman, 'Who Was the Real Princess Margaret' (*Vogue*, 17 November 2020), https://www.vogue.in/culture-and-living/content/the-crown-season-4-netflix-helena-bonham-carter-on-princess-margaret.

14 Rebecca Nicholson, 'Stargazing: Why Millennials Are Turning to Astrology' (*The Guardian*, 2018), https://www. theguardian.com/global/2018/mar/11/star-gazing-why-millennials-are-turning-to-astrology.

15 Christina Smallwood, 'Astrology in the Age of Uncertainty' (*The New Yorker*, 28 October 2019), https://www.newyorker.

com/magazine/2019/10/28/astrology-in-the-age-of-uncertainty.

16 Erin Griffith, 'Venture Capital Is Putting Its Money Into Astrology' (*The New York Times*, 15 April 2019), https://www.nytimes.com/2019/04/15/style/astrology-apps-venture-capital.html.

17 Ida C.Benedetto, 'Astrology Isn't Fake—It's Just Been Ruined By Modern Psychology' (*Quartz*, 3 January 2018), https://qz.com/1170481/horoscopes-2018-astrology-isnt-fake-its-just-been-ruined-by-modern-psychology/.

18 Jessa Crispin, 'I Love Astrology But the Current Craze Has It Wrong' (*The Guardian*, 30 January 2020), https://www.theguardian.com/commentisfree/2020/jan/30/astrology-trend-self-help-memes.

19 Philip Ball, 'How Astrology Paved the Way for Predictive Analysis' (*The Guardian*, 11 January 2020), https://www.theguardian.com/science/2020/jan/11/how-astrology-paved-way-predictive-analytics.

20 Lisa M. Lipscomb, *On the Cusp of Legitimacy: Professionalisation in the Field of Astrology* (New School for Social Research, 2020).

15

Jyotish Ups Its Game: *Reinventing Jyotish for the New Millennium*

When astrology could undergo a popular resurrection in the West, where it was not as much a part of daily life as it was here, what would a similar phenomenon in India look like? For Jyotish, the evolution of its practice ended up being a consequence of a dynamic interaction between India and the rest of the world. Educated and non-resident Indians went back to their roots only to help Jyotish branch out much further than ever before. From B.V. Raman's extensive lectures and addresses abroad to K.N. Rao's highly rigorous approach to Jyotish, a new benchmark had been set by the late 1990s. While there were many who took astrology from India to the West, there were some who travelled from the West to India in search of it—two of them were Robert Svoboda and Hart Defouw.

Svoboda, who is the first Westerner to be certified to practise Ayurveda in India, graduated from the University of Poona, now Savitribai Phule Pune University, in 1980 where he studied Ayurveda and won many accolades as a student. Since then, he has written about Hinduism extensively, including on Jyotish, in books such as *The Greatness of Saturn: A Therapeutic Myth* in 1997 and *Light on Life* in 2000. Of these, the latter remains one of the most important English language works on the fundamentals of Jyotish. Written along with Hart Defouw, it takes a bird's eye of view of Jyotish and is the perspective of outsiders immersed in a tradition foreign to their culture.

Besides these, Indian diplomat Bipin Behari's work has also helped initiate educated and rational beginners into Jyotish. Behari's *Fundamentals of Vedic Astrology*, published by Lotus Press in 2004, is another popular work that breaks down Jyotish in a way that is not only esoteric but also intellectual.

But while these books helped raise consciousness in the early 2000s, there was an unlikely personality coming from a completely different background, who would contribute towards a greater revolution in Jyotish.

Born in 1953 in Jalandhar in Punjab, Komilla Virk was a Bollywood actress before she turned to astrology.[1] She grew up in Delhi in a liberal Sikh family and went on to study economics at the prestigious Lady Sri Ram

College. But attracted to the world of glamour, she moved to Bombay, the home of the Hindi film industry, in her early twenties. She was introduced in the movie *Ishq Ishq Ishq* (1974) by the Bollywood superstar, Dev Anand, and made appearances in star-studded movies like *Suhaag* (1979), *Nagin* (1976), and *Chori Mera Kaam* (1975) but was never really noticed. Dissatisfied with her career and burdened by broken relationships, she began confiding in a friend who was well-versed in astrology. He gave her larger perspective about her life and soon she realised her destiny was not in Bollywood but she had a philosophical and spiritual calling.

In 1982, she moved to London, to start over, and married a British man, becoming Komilla Sutton. She set up an Indian handicrafts store and would read palms on some days to make some extra money. She continued to study astrology in her personal capacity and soon started speaking about it for a local radio show. This led to an invitation to speak at the Astrological Lodge of London. However, the reception there was less than favourable as the attendees didn't think much of Jyotish.

Jyotish Gets Organised

A more significant break came when she spoke about it at the Astrological Association of Great Britain in 1995. The association, established in 1958, was a much more serious venture as it was also the oldest astrological association in the world. Buoyed by the interest shown by her audience, she decided to take Jyotish seriously and create awareness about it. In the next few years, she set up the British Association for Vedic Astrology (BAVA), wrote her first and most translated book, *Essentials of Vedic Astrology*, and began teaching Jyotish.[2] By 1997, Sutton's BAVA was the leader in arranging annual conferences for Jyotish where astrologers from across Europe were encouraged to attend. An average conference would start with a Navagraha Pooja or a prayer ritual. Then there would be workshops, lectures and a masterclass about advanced astrological topics.

Around the same time, Jyotish was picking up in the US as well. It was the American Council of Vedic Astrology, set up a few years prior, that was the foremost voice in the country. It was modelled after B.V. Raman's ICAS and is now the largest network of Vedic astrologers around the world. His daughter, Gayatri Devi Vasudev, is amongst many who serve on its board. Anyone who wishes to get their certification can apply for the organisation's certifications that are obtained after training and an examination with a certified Jyotishi. Or one could attend classes at the American College of Vedic Astrology, where Sutton also teaches a course. A man central to both of these enterprises, Dennis Harness, also further set up the Sedona Vedic Astrology conference in 2013, organised annually in the state of Arizona. It is now one of the most popular of its kind—its 2020 edition took place virtually and had discussions on topics such as 'Language as the therapeutic tool of Jyotish', 'Poetry of the Grahas' and 'Jyotish in the Bhagavad Gita' among others.

Jyotish and YouTube

But while conferences and associations were for astrologers to gather and discuss their ideas, it was YouTube that brought Jyotish to lay enthusiasts. This was largely due to one man, Kapiel Raaj Srivastava, who set up his *KRSChannel—Learn Astrology* in 2009 and has posted two to three videos every week without fail ever since. With over 2,500 videos and over 400,000 subscribers today, his is possibly the most popular astrological channel on YouTube.

Right off the bat, he is everything one doesn't expect an Indian astrologer to be. In fact, he is diametrically opposite to an average Jyotishi in his persona. He shows up in his videos wearing sunglasses and expensive watches. He frequently talks about his love for meat, cigars and alcohol. He doesn't seem to take himself too seriously and is often light-hearted and sarcastic on camera. His take on Jyotish is savvy and may even feel subversive to a more conservative audience.

Born in New Delhi, he moved to the US with his family at the age of twelve. Like Sutton, he, too, was enamoured by the camera, growing up, and wanted to become a filmmaker. So, when an astrologer told him he was going to become an astrologer too, he brushed it off. Srivastava went on to study filmmaking and made several feature-length and short movies independently. But then came a low phase. At this time, incidentally a Saturn transit, he didn't even have twenty dollars to his name, and was cleaning kindergarten toilets and classrooms for a year because there was no other job available. Then the light of Jyotish dawned upon him.

Srivastava often mentions in his videos how he used to go online to read more about his astrological placements, only to find them inadequate or stereotypical nonsense. His uncle back in India was an astrologer and for about three years he spent hours on the phone learning Jyotish from him. He also read the works of B.V. Raman, K.N. Rao and others, and embraced astrology in every possible way.[3]

But he also saw how much Jyotish needed to be modernised, and set out on a mission to educate. For someone who didn't learn Jyotish the traditional way, it follows that his approach to teaching it would be non-traditional too. He speaks in accented English and films in different outdoor and indoor locations every now and then. He is also vocal about astrologers getting things wrong and advises his audience against believing them blindly. He doesn't prescribe expensive remedies and swears that he doesn't looks at his own and his family's charts. In his view, astrology is '25% technique, 25% intuition, 10% omens and 40% practice'.[4]

His videos are now the go-to source for many Jyotish enthusiasts, Indian and non-Indian alike. He also analyses current affairs astrologically as well as horoscopes of famous people. He conducts online discussions with other Jyotishis from around the world, creating his own mini conferences in this way. Srivastava also takes questions from his viewers regularly and actively fosters a community around his brand. He does this by wearing shirts and shooting in his house's basement, both of which feature his channel's name and logo. He also has an online astrology school, Magha Vedic Astrology Academy, where courses on Jyotish range from $100 to over $300.

Combining his love for filmmaking and astrology, he has also produced short movies about the Grahas of Rahu and Ketu. Playing the main character in both—in the former, *Interview of Rahu*, he finds himself hallucinating and tries to understand the nature of Rahu's illusions. In the latter, *Meeting Ketu*, he is a troubled man seeking therapy and explores the importance of the wounds of the past that is the domain of Ketu.

While his approach may be frowned upon by more serious practitioners and enthusiasts, he is a modern-day Jyotish guru who gets through to the ordinary people in a way most Jyotishis cannot. His mission as an astrologer, he states, is to give Jyotish a heartbeat again and to make it easy, fun and adventurous for anyone who wants to know about the science of light.[5] His popularity, then, suggests the extent to which Jyotish has retained its mystique as well as India's enduring fascination with astrology.

Following his lead, more astrologers have since launched their YouTube channels. These channels cater to a variety of audiences, from non-Indians to various Indian regional communities such as Tamil and Telugu-speakers. From the basics of a chart to the range of astrological placements, these channels now serve as a marketing tool for many astrologers. Channels that cater mostly to an Indian audience will particularly address common Indian questions such as whether one should settle abroad, have a 'love marriage', and so on. People often leave their birth details in the comments section, seeking an answer to their query only to be told to contact the astrologer for a paid reading over email. YouTube, in effect, has changed the way Jyotish is conducted in India. Not only has it taken astrology online but people can now also understand the basics of Jyotish before they consult an astrologer. Before these channels, an average astrology client had no way to understand the astrologer's jargon and was often swept away by it for better or worse.

In fact, Jyotish-related YouTube channels don't belong just to Indian astrologers but quite a lot of them are by non-Indian Jyotishis too. Spread over different parts of the world, these Jyotishis interpret the discipline not just from a traditional perspective but add their own cultural and intellectual flavour to it too. In this way, Jyotish has been modernised and globalised in a way that is in stark contrast to how it was traditionally kept hidden from the masses and veiled in utmost secrecy for the most part in India. That has had its pros and cons; as such, easily available information is liable to misinterpretation and misuse as well, but it is undoubtedly a paradigm shift. Unlike Western astrology, however, there aren't many millennial Jyotishis, especially Indians. That is perhaps owing to their bad experiences with it as well as an inherent bias against what is considered traditional.

Sutton, who lives in San Francisco now, too launched her channel in 2016 with the help of her niece. She now posts videos about latest transits and astrological concepts, recording videos from her study at her home.

She also coordinates her clothing to the colour associated with whichever planet a particular video relates to. So, if she is talking about what the latest Mercury transit is like, she'll show up wearing shades of Mercury's colour, which is green. Unlike Srivastava, she is much more grounded in her exposition of Jyotish, both for astrologers and enthusiasts.

But that doesn't always work. Once while speaking at an event in India about the philosophy of Jyotish, she was told by a member of the audience that he didn't want to know the theory and just needed to know the techniques for making predictions. So, in her consultations, she first asks her clients, half of whom tend to be Indian and the other half non-Indians, if they know anything about astrology. Usually, they don't really know anything and are mostly looking for therapy in the form of astrological counsel. For this reason, she prescribes simple remedies like chanting mantras or visiting temples. This is something even her younger Indian clients living across the world are happy to do.

Sutton believes that an astrologer must be a fundamentally good person who is more of an observer of life rather than someone immersed in it. This means a calm mind, no emotional ups and downs, and definitely no complicated relationships. Both Srivastava and Sutton are full-time astrologers, teaching online astrology courses and giving consultations to people around the world. While Srivastava focuses more on daily life matters such as career, relationships, and so on, Sutton offers consultations about understanding one's chart psychologically as well as selecting Muhurtas.

She is also open to concepts from Western or tropical astrology but makes an important distinction between that and Jyotish—whereas the former is primarily concerned with looking at the psychological makeup of an individual, the latter is mostly about prediction. This delineation has been quite stark until now but is increasingly becoming blurred. That is due to the astrology of Nakshatras, the original basis of Jyotish.

Canada-based Dr Arjun Pai, who launched his YouTube channel a year after Sutton, focuses on the asterisms as they tend to reveal one's psychological make up. He relates them with various Hindu mythological stories that have been passed down for generations but whose connection to Nakshatras and Jyotish was lost somewhere down the line. So, even if newborns in a Hindu household are named according to their Moon Nakshatra, astrologers don't look at these while making predictions or reading a chart.

Dr Pai, however, is not a full-time professional astrologer and works in finance and tech. But his videos tend to be much longer, looking at how one's psyche is shaped according to one's Nakshatras, which he explains through the story associated with that asterism. People with a prominent Ashwini, then, may find themselves gravitating towards healing in some form or may simply have a healing presence, as the Nakshatra is ruled by the physicians of the Gods, the Ashwini Kumars. Since every chart shows Nakshatra placements for the ascendant as well as each of the nine Grahas, this gives a substantial nuance to one's psychology in the framework of Jyotish.

Jyotish and Apps

Dr Pai has also worked closely with Cosmic Insights, an app exclusively dedicated to Jyotish, for a couple of years, for astrological consultations. It was launched in December 2016 by the UK-based Niravta Mathur and the US-based Archana Patchirajan. The duo met at the meditation and yoga movement, Art of Living.

Patchirajan, an engineer and entrepreneur, started studying astrology in 2014 following a personal tragedy. She found her answers, but her journey with the stars would continue. Teaming up with Mathur, who had worked in fashion and meditation before, for PR and marketing, she decided to write the code for a Jyotish-specific app. This was tricky because it had to reflect the daily lunar movements, since Jyotish is largely based on one's Moon, Nakshatra. However, since then the app has been developed to be comprehensive enough that it can now fully replace a desktop software for Jyotish. It incorporates Jyotish traditions of Parashara, Nadi, Jaimini and Tajik, as well as South Indian astrology that includes concepts such as Panchpakshi.

The app lets you save birth charts of friends and family, ask questions on the in-app forum and read about your astrological placements and the daily Panchang as it relates to you. However, Cosmic Insights is primarily geared towards the astrologer with a host of advanced features. For the enthusiasts, there is align27. It is much easier to understand as it not only shows the latest transits according to one's Moon, Nakshatra, but also explains what it means for them. It also seeks to help with time management by classifying one's days into three categories—green day, amber day and red day, and encouraging people to work and rest in accordance with how apt that time is for productivity, silence, conflict, etc.

Mathur and Patchirajan plan to roll out align27 as a wellness tool for corporates, where employees can be given a break when their personal quality of time is not so good and can be given added responsibilities if their stars are, in fact, aligned for that.

Patchirajan believes that artificial intelligence is the future of astrology because one cannot have access to a computer all the time to find out the latest transits. But even more importantly, astrology is not meant to be a tool for prediction solely, but can be better used for self-discovery. For this, one doesn't need daily advice from an astrologer, and an app can do the job instead. To help their audience, the founders work on making their content as positive and authentic as possible, so that even a difficult transit may be used productively. However, this is somewhat more popular with the Western users at the moment, even though many Indians have caught on as well.

A yearly subscription to *Cosmic Insights* costs about US$ 50 and a lifetime subscription, US$ 200, almost the same as the price of an astrology software. align27, on the other hand, costs US$ 80 for a year and US$ 250 for a lifetime subscription. The Indian consumer, used to getting his or her astrological predictions at a few hundred rupees at most, will probably take longer to accept this expensive model where accuracy matters more than the mental comfort of having sought an astrological consultation.

However, both the apps and their websites are easy on the eye and have a decidedly millennial friendly tone. So, when there was a conjunction of six Grahas in Capricorn in February 2021, a blog post by Patchirajan boiled it down in a way anyone could understand.[6] Published as 'Cosmic Conversations' on the *Cosmic Insights* website, it had Shani playing the party pooper. Since the planet rules the sign of Capricorn, as the party host he went around telling other planets to behave properly. With Surya, the Sun-father with whom he didn't have a good relationship, he launched into a tirade about how light and darkness are the same. He tells off Guru, the Jupiter-teacher, to stop preaching for a while. The softer planets of Buddha and Shukra, i.e., Mercury and Venus, feel confused and lost. At some point during this party conversation, Shani proclaims 'my home, my rules' to which everyone responds in emojis. Astrology in India has never been distilled like this and this is where inroads may be made with younger or uninitiated consumers.

Some of their other challenges, however, are rather comical. More than half of their negative reviews on the app stores are about people complaining about their Sun signs being incorrect. Since most people, Indians included, only know their Western astrology Sun sign, they end up feeling lost when Jyotish tells them that it's actually the sign prior to that which is their Sun sign. So, a Capricorn in the Western system will be a Sagittarius according to Jyotish. This is because the Western system follows the tropical zodiac, whereas Jyotish follows the sidereal one. The difference between these two zodiacs is a result of the precession of the Earth's axis, and so, it changes the birth chart almost entirely. But because people usually don't know of this distinction, it ends up being confusing to them and may even cause an identity crisis. 'People get stuck and then you have to educate them about Jyotish.' Mathur adds, 'They need some proof to let go of that archetype but they often turn around after using the align27 app for a while.'

But where Mathur and Patchirajan aim to empower the Jyotish enthusiast through self-discovery, Anton Zvyagintsev's Yodha does it by giving astrological counsel within twenty-four hours. The app mimics the text chat box that is so ubiquitous now and feels miles away from the traditional astrological counsel. However, Yodha astrologers are based in Nepal.

Anton, a resident of Russia, was visiting the country when he was taken in by the culture as well as the astrology he experienced there. Since mobile phones and WhatsApp were far more common than telephonic conversations and emails by that time, he decided to go the app route too. He launched Yodha in 2013. In the next few years, Anton and his team would meet and vet over ten thousand astrologers, of whom only two hundred are on their roster now. Each of them works for eight hours a day and there are three different shifts. The recruitment process is meticulous to the point that during an astrologer's trial period, all of his answers are reviewed and approved by another astrologer.

Zvyagintsev says that their customers appreciate the accuracy of their astrologers who can answer a variety of questions about one's career, love, finance and more, for Rs 500 or a little over $6. He believes that astrology is important today because people are bombarded by many options in every aspect of their lives, and sometimes they need help in figuring out the right choice.

Jyotish and Discourse

Chennai-based Aswin Subramanyan is a young astrologer who is not only trying to bring different astrological traditions together but also develop an intellectual discourse with that. A finance professional, he is a fifth-generation astrologer. Having grown up around astrology, he was always aware of it but didn't take it seriously until 2014 when he started learning it. He began with Jyotish but in three years moved on to Hellenistic astrology and now studies Islamic astrology as well. He finds studying philosophy and other astrological systems not only complemented his knowledge of Jyotish but also enriched it. But while Subramanyan tries to approach his astrology as rationally as possible, he doesn't think one could make a pure science out of it. Neither does he believe one could measure or quantify astrology statistically—there is too much intuition at work and there are too many permutations and combinations to be explored in order to read a birth chart comprehensively.

Instead, he spends more of his time talking and writing about astrology. In 2018, he set up a digital magazine and a podcast, both named *Celestial Vibes*. The magazine is available to paid subscribers only, as it doesn't carry any advertisements. The podcast, however, is freely accessible on his YouTube channel of the same name and features a variety of discussions like 'Practice of Astrology in Alexandrian Era', 'Astrological Determinism in Indian Buddhism' and 'Pricing of Astrological Services', among over a hundred such episodes. His guests are academics researching astrology or astrologers themselves.

The point is to get astrologers from around the world and different traditions to write and talk about astrology critically. His approach, both intellectually and technologically, is novel and one of a kind for an Indian astrologer. But he is not too caught up in intellectualising astrology and instead feels the real problem to be the lack of respect for the astrologer. Indians can often abuse and sometimes even refuse to pay if the astrologer doesn't tell them what they want to hear, or if the predictions go wrong. The American audience, he says, is far more receptive and respectful. He credits the large astrological community there for elevating the discourse and creating awareness amongst the general public.

Whether this will change anytime soon or not remains to be seen, but after television, astrologers have swooped up YouTube as a mode of addressing their audience. Jyotishis of different traditions and languages regularly post videos about various astrological placements, as well as their take on the latest news headlines in the country. While this is mostly done to build a client base, it still points towards a never-seen-before relationship between

an astrologer, the enthusiast and the final consumer.
The Jyotishi is now a professional in India, even if not as
legitimised as a doctor and the like. A potential consumer
can follow the astrologer's social media accounts before
getting a consultation and can even post a public review
of it later on. This has the potential to democratise what
was previously the domain of priests and highly guarded
from the common public. It could possibly lead to its own
problems but it has definitely made it much harder for
unethical astrologers to misguide his or her clients.

Because astrology is unlikely to go away in the years
to come, it is perhaps a good sign that astrologers are
now working towards reinventing it for the twenty-first
century. That has meant reinterpreting it for a global
and secular audience as well as adapting to the prevalent
cultural norms of the society and the latest technological
advancements. But most importantly, these astrologers
remind audiences that Jyotish can be much more than
a tool for predicting one's material future. It can be a
tool for self-discovery from a spiritual perspective—it
can uncover one's Karmic past and how that might have
shaped one's current life, which can help in gaining a
larger perspective of one's place in the world. On the other
hand, it can also give people a greater agency about their
future by making them realise how nothing is ever set in
stone. For a country full of astrologers and impressionable
enquirers, that alone may be the most important thing
they need to understand about Jyotish.

Notes

1   Teena Singh, 'Starlet Turns Stargazer' (*The Tribune*, 22 July 2001), https://www.tribuneindia.com/2001/20010722/herworld.htm.

2   Garry Philipson, 'An Interview with Komilla Sutton' (*Skyscript*, year unknown), https://www.skyscript.co.uk/komilla.html.

3   Simon Chokoisky, 'An Interview with Kapiel Raaj' (*Jyotish Star*, 15 August 2015), https://www.jyotishstar.com/jyotish-star-kapiel-raj-september-2015.html.

4   Ibid.

5   Ibid.

6   Archana Patchirajan, 'Cosmic Conversation' (*Cosmic Insights*, 19 January 2021), https://blog.cosmicinsights.net/cosmic-conversation-sun-saturn-jupiter-and-mercury-in-capricorn/.

16

Researching Astrology: *Academia and Contemporary Thinkers*

After being rescued from Sun signs in the mainstream arena, astrology could finally open up to research. But that comes with its own set of challenges. Nicholas Campion, the world's foremost researcher and writer on astrology, was an astrologer before he ventured into academia. He took over the horoscope writing column started by R.H. Naylor from his son, John Naylor, at the beginning of his career. He wrote prolifically as an astrologer and eventually got into tracing the history and culture of astrology. His seminal work, *Astrology and Cosmology in the World's Religions*, was published by New York

University Press in 2012 and it remains an authoritative compendium on the topic. It is a comprehensive look at all astrological systems in the world, including those of the Native Americans and Indigenous Australians, and how they have influenced religion in their respective countries. He currently heads the master's programme in Cultural Astronomy and Astrology at the University of Wales Trinity Saint David in the UK.

The course was set up in 2008 at the time when Campion was working on his PhD at Bath University for which he looked at the extent and nature of contemporary belief in astrology. So, when a funding opportunity to create a course came up, he applied for it and the course was initially started at Bath itself. It was later shifted to its current location, but it remains a one-of-its-kind accredited academic degree by a university.

It explores the relationship between cosmology and culture, drawing on disciplines such as history, anthropology, archaeology, sociology, philosophy and theology. It also includes the study of relationships between the soul, the psyche and the cosmos, as well as ancient practices of magic and divination. It's an online-only programme that admits at most sixty students at a time, with a full-time and a part-time curriculum. The students are awarded a Master of Arts degree following a supervised fifteen-thousand-word dissertation. Some of the recent dissertations by students include ones on the practice of Navagraha rituals amongst the Indian community in the UK and a study of the night sky in a Canadian town where electric lights had been switched off.

An overwhelming majority of the students are women, and more than half of them are astrology enthusiasts. They come from various backgrounds such as astrophysics, physics, history, anthropology, theatre, and more. A select few also come in trying to understand the history of astronomy from a wider perspective. Despite the success of the programme, Campion, however, is not too optimistic about astrology in academia. Even if one were to set up more such courses, he says, there weren't more than ten scholars in all of UK with the combination of astrological knowledge and academic rigour to design one.

'Studying astrology critically can help us uncover insights into ancient civilisations and its distinction with astronomy is only a modern Western phenomenon,' he points out. As a historian, Campion supports ventures such as Project Hindsight as they made English translations of medieval astrological texts available for the first time and is surprised by the lack of academic research into Jyotish, given its prevalence amongst Indian communities, as well as the lack of educational courses in it.

Jeffrey Kotyk, on the other hand, has focused on the history and transmission of astrology amongst various Asian and medieval systems as part of his broad research field. Based in Canada, Kotyk studied Buddhism at university before he went on to do his PhD in Buddhist Astrology and Astral Magic with the Tang Dynasty in 2017 at the Leiden University. For this, he explored how astrological systems of India, Iran and the Hellenistic world played a significant role in the development of Buddhism while China's Tang Dynasty was in power between the seventh and tenth centuries. While Indian astrology was available to the Chinese even prior to that, it was only in the eighth century that it became an important part of Chinese Buddhism, which further affected the development of the religion in the East Asia region. As a result, many astrological texts from around the world were translated in China at the time and eventually, Iranian astrology became more prevalent than Indian. Kotyk examines the transmission of horoscopy and lunar mansions amongst different astrological systems, both of which were significant to the cultural life of Chinese Buddhists. He continues to examine the transcultural history between China and the world as a research fellow at the University of British Columbia. He often uses his Twitter account to share his findings with his followers, including those related to astrology. So, whether it's sharing the Chinese version of the Nakshatra Purusa, or the lunar mansion man, or various ways in which Saturn is personified in Asia, he regularly interacts with fellow academics and enthusiasts alike over such material. Kotyk believes that a lot of ancient and medieval iconography and lore are lost when we refuse to study astrology academically. However, the problem is unlikely to be resolved anytime soon because none of the science, religion and history departments at the universities seem to want anything to do with astrology. Grants are also hard to come by as people don't want their donations to be used to fund 'superstition'.

'Many people believe in destiny without believing in astrology,' he points out. People love to talk about fate and determinism, waxing eloquent about the significant role these might have played in their lives, but do not entertain astrology as a means to inspect this fate and fortune. Many don't realise that birth charts are extremely technical, unlike other forms of divination which are completely based on intuition. The fixedness of the stars, the Sun, the Moon and the planets gives astrology a timeless foundation while allowing for changing mores of the time to shape it age after age. It also gives astrology the status of a religion, especially in present times when organised religion is on the decline.

In recent years, there haven't been more than thirty such scholars across the world who have engaged in academic research on astrology. Kotyk, however, believes that number may go up as now there is an increased availability of astrological texts. Astrologers can now communicate across traditions and communities much more easily, which in turn helps those who research it as well. The Indian astrological community can interact with the Italian, or the Iranian with the Buddhist, making the real-time discourse on astrology quicker and more wide-ranging than ever before.

Then there are the likes of Stephane Gerson, director at the Institute of French Studies at New York University in the US, who wrote about the famous astrologer Nostradamus as a cultural and historical phenomenon. His book, *Nostradamus: How an Obscure Renaissance Astrologer Became the Modern Prophet of Doom*, was published in 2012 and is an in-depth biography of the man. The same year, Gerson also co-edited a Penguin Classics edition of Nostradamus' *The Prophecies*, which is the seminal work the French astrologer is most known for. It contains over nine hundred prophecies by him, written in the form of quatrains or four-line poems, even though during the course of his life he is believed to have made more than six thousand prophecies. While he started out as an apothecary in plague-infested France in the sixteenth century, he eventually started writing almanacs to supplement his income. They took off beyond his expectations but the reason his name still endures is because of people who are either his fans or occult-inclined conspiracy theorists. In the aftermath of major world events, such as the 9/11 attacks in New York City, email chains circulated a fake six-line poem which was cited as a prediction by him:

> Two steel birds will fall from the sky on the Metropolis
> The sky will burn at forty-five degrees latitude
> Fire approaches the great new city
> Immediately a huge, scattered flame leaps up
> Within months, rivers will flow with blood
> The undead will roam the earth for little time. [1]

Because of this, the sales for Nostradamus' *Les Propheties*, originally published by him in 1555, shot up in 2001 on Amazon and books related to him became bestsellers. Similarly, his name has been associated with other events such as the French Revolution, the American Civil War, the deaths of German leader Adolf Hitler and the American President John F. Kennedy, the bombing of Hiroshima and Nagasaki in Japan, and more. [2] In India, a Nostradamus prediction was splashed across social media to show how he had predicted the victory of the current Indian prime minister, Narendra Modi, and the defeat of the incumbent Congress Party in 2014.[3] Suffice it to say that his works are routinely misinterpreted and misrepresented for when people want to understand a shocking world event, gain legitimacy for their biases and theories through such 'prophecies', or are just that enthralled by astrology in general and want to force-fit Nostradamus' predictions to as many events as possible. In any case, the phenomenon of Nostradamus in popular culture makes it abundantly clear as to what happens when astrological literature is not handled with the erudition and integrity of a scholar.

Looking at History Astrologically

Where academic researchers have their hands tied in a sense, Richard Tarnas was not bound by such limitations and allowed his imagination to take flight when he wrote *Cosmos and Psyche*. A cultural historian, he attended Harvard University in 1968 where his interest in cosmology was first ignited. That led him to the Esalen Institute in California where he studied psychotherapy with the prominent Czech psychiatrist Stanislav Grof between 1974 and 1984. Grof's experiments with psychotherapy involved LSD where he has documented records of patients undergoing an expanded consciousness of the cosmos and he has also spoken about his own experiences with synchronicity extensively. Tarnas, after working with Grof, wrote two books, *The Passion of the Western Mind* and *Prometheus the Awakener*, which were a prequel to what he really wanted to say with *Cosmos and Psyche* in 2006.[4]

Tarnas believes there is something fundamentally lacking in the modern Western worldview and lists three ways in which it shows up. Firstly, he writes that the contemporary human experience is characterised by a profound metaphysical disorientation and a lack of solid foundation. He alludes to the absence of a larger order of purpose and significance, a guiding metanarrative that transcends cultures and a sense of meaning that could give the collective human society a nourishing coherence and intelligibility. Next, he addresses the deep sense of alienation that affects the modern self. And finally, he recognises the unfulfilled human and societal need for a deeper insight into one's unconscious forces and tendencies, whether creative or destructive, that play an important role in shaping our lives.

He also makes an elaborate distinction between the mind of the primal human and the modern one. The primal world, Tarnas points out, communicated, had purpose, and was full of signs, symbols, implications and intentions. The external world reflected the internal psychological world of humans, so there was a sense of continuity and flow, with a meaning both human and cosmic. The modern mind, however, divides the experience between the subjective human self and the objective external world. Their cosmos is impersonal and unconscious. Despite all the beauty in the world, the modern mind perceives the universe only as matter in motion, mechanistic, purposeless and ruled by chance and necessity. For this mind, the world that is external to the human being lacks conscious intelligence and meaning. In fact, the modern mind considers the primal one as misguided in conflating the inner and the outer, which caused the ancients to live in a 'state of continuous magical delusion'. The real experience and meaning lies in human consciousness alone, for the modern individual. Astrology, he writes, is the last lingering vestige of primitive animism, a strangely enduring affront to the objective rationality of the modern mind.

This difference, he points out, did not instantly arise in the seventeenth century but was a process that was thousands of years in the making. The new world was no longer subject to powers that be, Gods and Goddesses, or sacred ends, but a neutral domain of facts. The disenchanted modern world allowed the modern human being to depersonalise everything outside of him or her, fit to be exploited for one's benefit and self-interest, bringing on new challenges such as ecological crises and endemic poverty that is not dislodged by the world's growing prosperity.

For his research, he looked at astrological transits and the historical figures and events that corresponded those transits. He looks at planets as Jungian archetypes and found the Saturn archetype, for instance, to be akin to a stopped watch. It involves 'interrelated themes of stoppage and being stuck (in both mind and watch), of opposition and rejection, error, fault, corrections, judgement and self-judgement'. Looking at planetary transits for individuals, he goes into their Saturn Returns. The German composer,

Beethoven, for instance, released his first major work, the First Symphony, at the age of thirty. Figures like Shakespeare, Kepler and Galileo achieved major professional milestones, Marie Curie discovered radium and Niels Bohr formulated his theory of atomic structure, and Martin Luther King was arrested for protesting racial segregation which was to become his legacy later. He lists literary references where writers from Gertrude Stein to Tennessee Williams refer to the time between the ages of twenty-eight and thirty as the time of growing up into an adult, where they are obviously unaware of the Saturn Return archetype themselves. He mentions Jung here as well, because it was during this time period in his life that he first wrote to Freud, which ended up shaping his professional legacy decisively.

The planets of Uranus, Neptune and Pluto are believed to be intense and disruptive energies, associated with change, rebellion, freedom, sudden flashes of freedom, and so on. In fact, the discovery of Uranus in 1781 was in itself a disruption of the five-planet model of humanity that was prevalent until then. Tarnas draws parallels to the myth of Prometheus and links Uranus' astrological meaning and the signing of the Declaration of Independence, the revolt against aristocracy throughout the Western world, beginning of feminist movements and the varied technological advances of the time. While the planet was named after the Greek God Ouranos, the God of 'the starry sky' and the father of Cronos, the mythical counterpart of Saturn, Tarnas believes its astrological meaning is more relevant to the figure of Prometheus to which he dedicated his second book. Neptune, discovered in 1846, is associated with transcendent spirituality, sea and water. Here Tarnas finds parallels with the growing spiritualism in the world in the late 1840s, ascendancy of idealist and romantic philosophies, new interest in both Eastern mystical and Western esoteric traditions in the West, and finally, the emergence of theosophy. Finally, there is Pluto that was discovered in 1930. Believed to rule the 'Underworld', it is associated with the principles of power, depth and intensity. It can be catastrophic, overwhelming and destructive. Once again, we may note how the early twentieth century brought world wars, the rise of modern industrial civilisation and other major societal changes. Tarnas believed the transits of planets like Jupiter, Saturn, Uranus, Neptune and Pluto with longer orbital revolutions were more reliable predictors of historical trends than those that were shorter like Mercury's. For example, he noted the alignments of Uranus and Pluto often yielded revolutionary events like the invention of the printing press by Gutenberg, the stirrings of the French Revolution (the decade from 1787 to 1798) and significant political upheavals between 1845-1856 all around the world—a snapshot reveals the drafting of Karl Marx's *Communist Manifesto*, the Indian Sepoy Mutiny, the fall of the Tokugawa system in Japan, the break up of the Ottoman Empire and the incipient stirrings of feminism.

Next up in the 1960s, during such a conjunction, the world saw the Vietnam War, Chinese Cultural Revolution and the hippie movement, among other events. Tarnas refers to a Rolling Stone song—'Street Fighting Man'—to exemplify how the transit manifested in the Western psyche—'Hey! Said my name is called disturbance/I'll shout and scream, I'll kill the king, I'll rail at all his servants.' This decade saw the US and Russia launch human in space programmes with Apollo and Vostok respectively, where the former had Neil Armstrong walk on the Moon and the latter had Yuri Gagarin orbit around the Earth in his space capsule.

When it comes to transits of Saturn and Pluto, he found resonances of it in the two world wars and the 9/11 terrorist attack in New York City. Unlike the previous alignment, this has been seen to be a graver transit because of what Saturn represents astrologically. These periods also saw the rise of Nazism, the rise of Japanese militarism, the beginning of mass starvation of seven million Ukrainians by the Soviet ruler Joseph Stalin, mass killings of Armenians by Ottoman Turks, and more. Even the year 2020 that saw an unprecedented series of events, including millions of Coronavirus-related deaths, was marked by a Saturn and Pluto conjunction. Other than this, these alignments also mark economic difficulties such as the one in October 1929 that saw 'the blackest day in stock market history', and the Great Depression.

Jupiter and Uranus alignments, however, seem to be the harbinger of positive and enriching changes. It is a conjunction that occurs every fourteen years and has seen events such as the demonstration of the telescope by Galileo Galilei, the public announcement of Charles Darwin's theory of evolution, and more. In a 1920-21 transit of the two planets, Albert Einstein's theory of relativity was accepted by the scientific community and consequently launched the domains of quantum mechanics and nuclear physics. Tarnas notes that Einstein's own chart reflects a similar alignment and so his life was emblematic of the combined energies of Jupiter and Uranus—'the supremely successful intellectual breakthrough, the astonishing leap of the scientific imagination beyond the established structures of time and space, the scarcely conceivable sudden shift in the nature of reality and the celebrated and honoured rebel genius.'

To the alignment of Uranus and Neptune, Tarnas associates not just spiritualism in general but also spiritually inspired political activism, such as that of Mahatma Gandhi. When the Indian resistance leader wrote to the Russian writer Leo Tolstoy on the topic in 1909-10, it was under the auspices of this alignment that the correspondence took place. At this time, Sri Aurobindo, the venerated Indian monk, established the Pondicherry ashram, which is now the symbol of alternative and sustainable living in the modern capitalistic model.

Tarnas looks into many more such alignments and events that correspond to them, but is also careful to clarify that these events did not happen as a result of a switch being turned on or off, but were culminations of larger historical trends. That they tended to precipitate around certain planetary alignments is where he wants to draw the readers' attention. The changes seen during these years left an enduring impact even on the modern mind, and may lead to more such shifts in the near future. He emphasises that investigating something as infinitely complicated and mysterious as human history, or even a single human life, can never be neatly comprehended by any theoretical structure. In his research, he had moments where there was no apparent astrological connection, but with a deeper grasp of the astrological principles at work, he'd come upon insights. While he writes that he made disciplined effort at not force-fitting his theory to the data, one may still find his work to be a case of confirmation bias to a great extent, if not entirely so. However, if there is even a modicum of truth to the parallels drawn by him, then his ideas are worth pondering over. It may also be likened to the astrological idea of ages such as the Age of Aquarius which is currently the talk of the town in astrological circles. While no one can agree on whether it has already started or if we are heading towards it, many claim that the modern world's shift towards spirituality, innovations in Artificial Intelligence (AI) and the potentiality of space travel are Aquarian themes. Given that astrology, by and large, cannot be measured in terms of scientific empiricism, Tarnas' work perhaps serves more as a musing than a provable hypothesis. It tries to follow the astrological dictum of 'as above, so below' in forming its narrative, even though the astrological claim that our lives and the epochs of humanity are subject to repetitive patterns will forever remain a contested one.

Hindu Mythology and Astrological Archetypes

But researching astrology need not require one to understand or be interested in astrology. That was the case with the Sri Lankan Tamil writer Ananda Coomaraswamy who looked into astrological iconography in his essay, *The Iconography of Sagittarius.*[5] Coomaraswamy is best known for his 1918 book, *Dance of Shiva,* which introduced Indian art and its underlying philosophy to the West and inspired thinkers across the world. The essay now appears with some of his other unpublished work in the book, *Guardians of the Sundoor,* which is an eclectic exploration of similar themes from Hindu, Greek and Egyptian mythology. In a letter to his wife on the progress of this work, he wrote, 'Moira as will and destiny [...] corresponds to Dharma, of which each one's allotment is his sva-dharma, vocation, the natural means of his entelechy [or realisation of potential].' After this, he explained that Karma represented the 'ineluctable operation of mediate causes' which could hinder our destiny, but our only escape from it was to submit to it.

With Sagittarius, he wanted to understand what the centaur, or the half man-half horse, was shooting his arrow at and what he was defending. He believed the Sagittarian archer to be none other than the character of Krsanu from Rig Veda, who was associated with the constellation of Tisya, now known as Pushya. He once stood guard at a Hindu religious sacrifice and shot an arrow at a falcon flying overhead, and so, Krsanu is also associated with Agni or fire. Coomaraswamy traces the various references to this figure in other Hindu texts, and his analysis may be more cultural anthropology than a study of astrological iconography. That the Nakshatra of Pushya is associated with the zodiac of Sagittarius even in the modern Jyotish framework speaks about the consistency of the stories of Nakshatras and their connection to Hindu mythology.

Coomaraswamy passed away before he could explore his ideas more deeply and comprehensively. But while these iconographies may feel ostentatiously astrological in their appearance, an investigation of these may yield insights far beyond astrology itself. The modern research around astrology, then, is not only about getting a deeper sense of human history by studying the astrological iconography but also about developing an astrological narrative of the human history. Whether this will yield substantial insights years down the line or enhance our understanding of the world we live in or not, it is here to stay in one form or the other. That is so because it is impossible to separate astrology from the human experience, whether in the current century or even in a futuristic age, as it has been a building block of collective human knowledge.

Notes

1   Jimmy Akin, *Nostradamus: Astrologer? Prophet? Psychic?* (Jimmy Akin, 2021), https://www.youtube.com/watch?v=BvcaNG3jjsM.

2   Aine Cain, '9 Famous Predictions by Nostradamus that Some People Say Foresaw Future' (*Business Insider*, 21 March 2018), https://www.businessinsider.in/strategy/9-famous-predictions-by-nostradamus-that-some-people-say-foresaw-the-future/articleshow/63388883.cms.

3   FP Staff, 'Nostradamus: Did He Really Predict Modi's Victories, Hindutva's Rise and Sonia Gandhi's Fall' (*Firstpost*, 29 March 2017), https://www.firstpost.com/india/nostradamus-predicted-modis-victories-hindutvas-rise-sonia-gandhis-fall-3357952.html.

4   Chris Brennan, 'Richard Tarnas on Cosmos and Psyche' (*The Astrology Podcast*, 2020), https://www.youtube.com/watch?v=JTdwE_qVTE0.

5   Anand Coomaraswamy, *Guardians of the Sundoor* (Fons Vitae, 2004).

17

Future of Astrology:
To Be or Not to Be?

The question perpetually lingers in one's mind—should astrology be part of our lives? It might be helpful to borrow some perspective from the *Autobiography of a Yogi*, a celebrated work of Hindu philosophy by Indian monk Paramahansa Yogananda. Published in 1946, it is not just Yogananda's life history, but also an account of his meetings with the spiritual figures of both the Eastern and the Western world as well as his travels in the US where he spoke at length about Kriya Yoga. It was one of the favourite reads of Apple founder Steve Jobs.

Chapter sixteen of the book, 'Outwitting the Stars',

records Yogananda's conversations about astrology with his guru, Sri Yukteswar Giri. It starts with the guru, asking his disciple to get an astrological amulet, to which the latter remarks that he doesn't believe in astrology, but should he? The guru, then, responds, 'Charlatans have brought the stellar science to its present state of disrepute.' He continues by remarking how astrology is 'too vast, both mathematically and philosophically, to be rightly grasped except by men of profound understanding' and that 'ignoramuses' misreading the heavens, seeing scrawls and instead of scripts, was an undesirable but expected outcome.

The guru launches into a philosophical discussion about how human life is inextricably linked to everything in the universe. The planets and the stars, he says, are not benevolent or malevolent in and by themselves, but merely represent certain vibrations. He evokes the principle of Karma in saying that these heavenly influences merely 'offer a lawful channel for the outward operation of cause-effect equilibriums, which each man has set into motion in the past'.

Like Kepler, he believes that a child is born on the day and the hour when the universe reflects his or her individual Karma. The birth chart, then, contains both one's unalterable past and the probable future, but there are very few who can adequately interpret these. However, instead of taking a fatalistic view, he takes a more proactive one in emphasising that one is not a slave to one's past life actions. Since it was one's soul that instigated certain actions, the same soul can overcome their results through spiritual resolve. Like Vivekananda, he too denounces the 'superstitious awe of astrology [that] makes one an automaton, slavishly dependent on mechanical guidance'. The wise individual, he says, 'defeats his [or her] planets'. The soul is beholden to the Spirit, or the Brahman, not the stars.

In order to do this, the guru expounded self-realisation and breaking out of one's compulsive psychological and behavioral patterns. Answering the student's question regarding the utility of obtaining an amulet, Giri remarks that astrological remedies like wearing a certain stone or metal can help contract one's 'bad' Karma. He later tells Yogananda the reason for initiating this conversation with him—the stars, he tells his disciple, were about to take an unfriendly interest in him and cause health issues in a month's time. While the issues may persist for six months, with the amulet they may last only for twenty-four days.

So the disciple does as advised by his guru and gets the amulet. When the illness shows up, Yogananda is surprised and reports excruciating pain in his liver. On the twenty-third day of this 'torture', he chooses to travel to his guru who had left for Varanasi in the meanwhile. Upon meeting him, he is asked by his guru to exercise. When he speaks of his pain at doing so, the guru trumps him by saying, 'You say you have pain; I say you have none. How can such contradictions exist?'

Yogananda has a moment of insight at this point. While the destined illness did show up, he made his experience of it worse by feeling enslaved to it. Pain and distress, then, were psychological for the most part and the sheer awareness of that helped alleviate much. He recounts the time he burnt his horoscope when it was prophesised that he would marry thrice in his life. While he never actually married, his family did try to arrange his marriage thrice. He would turn it down every time, insisting on his overwhelming love for the divine.

'The deeper the self-realisation of a man, the more he influences the whole universe by his subtle spiritual vibrations, and the less he himself is affected by the phenomenal flux,' he reiterates his guru's words at the end of the chapter.

We may also borrow words of wisdom from Fritjof Capra, the Austrian-born American physicist and author of the wildly successful book, *The Tao of Physics*. Published in 1975, it has sold millions of copies worldwide and has been translated in more than twenty languages to date. Capra draws parallels between modern physics and Eastern thought, believing both to be highly compatible with the other.

He believed that while scientific research was driven by rational knowledge and activities, there was also an element of intuitive insights that seemingly come out of nowhere.[1] He cites the examples of Niels Bohr and Werner Heisenberg who were influenced by ideas in Chinese and Hindu thought respectively. Both of them worked on quantum mechanics which points towards an atomic interconnectedness in the universe.

Capra believes that this interconnectedness can be found in Eastern thought in ideas of Taoism and Advaita Vedanta. He draws on many myths and texts from the

East to present his case throughout the book. While physicists of other schools of thought have criticised his approach in the past, it is his conclusion that feels most thought-provoking. He writes, 'I see science and mysticism as two complementary manifestations of the human mind; of its rational and intuitive faculties. The modern physicist experiences the world through an extreme specialisation of the rational mind; the mystic through an extreme specialisation of the intuitive mind. The two approaches are entirely different and involve far more than a certain view of the physical world. However, they are complementary. Neither is comprehended in the other, nor can either of them be reduced to the other, but both of them are necessary, supplementing one another for a fuller understanding of the world. Science does not need mysticism, and mysticism does not need science, but men and women need both. Mystical experience is necessary to understand the deepest nature of things, and science is essential for modern life. What we need, therefore, is not a synthesis but a dynamic interplay between mystical intuition and scientific analysis.'[2]

The scientist in Capra probably did not have astrology in mind when he wrote about Eastern mysticism, but this worldview of his can still be useful when approaching the discipline. Notwithstanding the commonplace practice of astrology throughout the ages, it is worth remembering that it is the same primal impulse to understand the nature of life that has guided many on the astrological path since time immemorial. There is no apparent connection between astrology and quantum physics on the surface, but underlying that, there is the common intuition of the interconnectedness of everything. Where physicists observe it at the minutest physical level as atoms, the mystics do so on the scale of a seemingly incomprehensible cosmic web of fate and Karma. In the totality of this, as Capra illustrates, lies the human experience. The entirety of this human experience does not lend itself to language, human constructs of logic and rationality, and empirical measurement. Even something as pervasive as love, be it familial or romantic, may be difficult to explain rationally, but countless people since the advent of humanity have sworn by it. For years, they have performed, and continue to perform, unimaginable feats in the service of it everyday around the world.

At this point, it may be necessary to recognise the distinction between the history of intellectual thought and the history of humanity itself. When the ancient humans began to deify the Sun, Moon, planets and stars, it was for a variety of purposes. It gave them calendars, helped fix authority for their human rulers and priests, manage cultural and religious lives, and more. This proved to be so useful that our lives still revolve around the structures they set up. But beyond this, their deep personification of the celestial heavyweights was not just idle superstition. Rather, it helped them understand, confront and accept the humanity within them. They needed to understand tendencies such as pride, emotions, the importance of intellect and writing, aggression and cruelty, love of pleasure, wisdom, rejection and hardships, because they were a part of their daily life, just like ours today. Unlike us, they had no need to separate their humanity from the cosmos. In fact, they actively found ways to connect the two in whatever they did. This gave the average human being a sense of belonging to life, in which everything was sacred and full of meaning. No matter what one's subconscious and unconscious presented, it could be understood externally, without hassle. That is in sharp contrast to modern life where we consider ourselves much more progressive and enlightened and yet struggle to understand and accept diversity of thought when it comes to religion, politics, gender, and more.

In this context, it might be helpful to look at astrology as a mental model. It helps navigate something complicated, such as the nature of our existence and destiny, through something approximate, such as astrological principles and a birth chart. It was developed as such by generations of priests, cultural astronomers and astrologers who made a variety of observations and measurements, drawing parallels between celestial movements and events around them. To make this model easier to grasp, the celestial bodies were treated as deities rather than physical bodies. However, this process of observing, recording and writing down the apparent correlations between the heavens and the Earth was subject to individual biases, judgement and limitations, as imposed by pre-existing mores of the times they lived in. In addition to that, since these correlations were abstractions and approximations to begin with, astrology cannot be expected to be precise in an empirical sense. Of course, that means astrology can often fail at fulfilling what is considered its promise—predicting your future with complete accuracy and certainty. Astrologers differ on the reasons for the gaps and the steps to be taken to correct them.

Be that as it may, it is rarely noted that the astrologer of today is radically different from the astrologer of premodern times in one crucial way—the astrologer is not an astronomer and a mathematician anymore. That not only creates a crisis of legitimacy for the astrologer's work but possibly affects its accuracy and understanding of the cosmos vis-a-vis life on Earth as well. Since astrology began as a system of observation-based correlations, one wonders as to why astrologers have abdicated the basic premise of their craft and only rely on texts written centuries ago. While researching older texts, reinterpreting them for the current realities and approaching the work with integrity may help astrologers, bringing mathematical skill and astronomy may help refine some outdated astrological concepts and formulate new ones.

However, even in its existing form, astrology has its own utility. We can look at the planetary and stellar deities as archetypes or stories that are at work not just in our own selves but also in people around us. This can help us break from the stranglehold of what is normal, which is nothing more than being well-adjusted to social norms of one's immediate environment and expand our understanding of human behaviour. So, instead of thinking someone to be too dominating, timid, friendly, ambitious or weird, we can think of them as embodying such archetypes. In doing so, we may discern one's inherent strengths and weaknesses better. While we often think that our current self is a result of upbringing and early life experiences, it is not well-recognised that what we take away from these formative ages is a result of inherent tendencies that we are born with. In order to overcome or augment these tendencies, we need to become aware of them first, and that's where astrological archetypes can play a role. They can not only illuminate contours of our lives, psychologically and materially, but also help us realise we are not alone in our experience of life.

How many times have you thought of a weakness as something you just can't rid yourself of because that's just who you are? Or that you do not seem to be able to kick a compulsive habit you formed because of something that happened years ago? Or didn't realise you had a certain strength or an inborn talent until someone pointed it out to you? Astrology can help broaden our perspective when it comes to such self-imposed limitations or unexplored possibilities that lie dormant in us.

At the same time, astrological archetypes can also help us navigate life situations. Often, when things are not going well and we feel life is beating us down for no apparent reason, we tend to fixate on the unfairness of it all. In such situations, it can be useful to think about Saturn. It is the planet that brings hardships in order to teach us a lesson about our past behaviour. On the other hand, when things are going great and there is an abundance of prosperity, pleasure and success, it might be good to stay level-headed and remember the Venusian archetype. The goodness and the pleasure it ushers into our life does not last forever, lest we start taking it for granted or get lost in the material world. Then there are times in life when all we need is a few moments of insane courage and self-belief. We can summon that in ourselves in a number of ways but also through the archetype of Mars. It is the planet that can go out and get whatever it wants through sheer determination and force. Alternatively, Mars can also be that instance of road rage we might find ourselves in or that aggressive and over-competitive co-worker.

Where Mercury could be the reading of an interesting book, Jupiter could be the wisdom we grasp upon its completion and contemplation. If we find our soul coming alive because of something we did in our life, perhaps it is our Sun. But at the same time, the Sun could also be that brilliant but excessively proud top-ranked student in the class. The Moon, on the other hand, touches us every day with its waxing and waning, causing mood swings in us. It also shows the hurt feelings whenever we go through any kind of pain in life. Finally, when we find ourselves drawn to situations and people for no apparent or logical reason, that's Rahu and Ketu at play.

In essence, we can make use of astrology at a personal level without practising or believing in it. As we already noted, there is much about the human experience that can be inexplicable and unnerving. The human unconscious further stores up much that can be disturbing or irrational for our conscious to process. This is where the birth chart can come in, as it can help us relate to our inner life from a completely new perspective. It can help us look at our impulses from a distance without abdicating the responsibility for the actions resulting from these impulses. Much of our lives are about navigating this unknown impulsive element in our subconscious and unconscious and the struggle that ensues on a daily basis. Unlike religious and political ideology, which tell us to suppress, fight or fix these impulses, astrology can help us accept them, and in doing so, resolve them. That is perhaps its most important and profound service in the modern world where an overemphasis on rationality and atheism has left a psychological void in our lives.

For this reason, it behooves both the believers and the sceptics to understand the possibilities and limitations of astrology. Believers may benefit more by remembering that while astrology can aid in the process of self-discovery and self-realisation, it does not have the last word on one's inner truths. It is the birth chart or the astrological principles that are supposed to adapt to the reality of one's life and not the other way round. Astrologers and thinkers of all stripes consistently stress upon being true to oneself. That means recognising and standing up for one's inner convictions, about how one should live their life as it relates to aspects of the self, relationships, work, and more. Believers should be able to use astrology to elevate their understanding of the self without making it a never-ending project of massaging one's ego. It is also worth recognising that perhaps the future is truly unknowable or cannot be predicted down to the minutest detail. In that case, it might be better to ease the reliance on astrology and take life as it comes.

The sceptics, on the other hand, may want to acknowledge the sheer adaptability and resilience of astrological thought. Its literature and tools have both found a way to adapt to the latest possible quality of life, whether it was the ancient world of the Mayans or the highly individualised and secular existence of a millennial in New York City. It speaks to the inherent utility and need for astrology in human life, for which it continues to survive. Every single individual in the world, whether a head of state of a powerful country or the poorest of the people in a remote island nation, will have a birth chart. Their story, whether objectively good or bad, is connected to that of the cosmos. As far as mental models go, it is greater than religion even, because unlike the divine, the chart can speak to you in clear and concise terms. It can give you explanations for your past and guidelines for the future that you can inculcate in your life easily. At the end of the day, perhaps the appeal of astrology lies in the fact that it can make us feel seen, which is more powerful than the blind faith of religion and the razor-sharp reason of rationality. And so, to summarily dismiss one of humanity's oldest and most enduring mental models based on a superficial or prejudiced investigation of it would be rather callous.

So, what does this mean for the future of astrology? Is this a story that will continue for ages still? That is something that only time can tell, but it might be interesting to remember the three Hollywood movies that were part of the series, The Matrix. Its 'red-pilled' humans of a society far, far more advanced than ours could download skills such as a new language or martial arts into their brains within a few seconds, but when it came to taking important life decisions, they still needed 'The Oracle'. This diviner of future was an old lady who did not read birth charts, palms, tarot cards or even tea leaves. But when people visited her for advice, she sometimes misled them deliberately, spoke in abstractions or predicted events that were too hard to believe for the characters in the movie. But whatever she did and said, she became an active agent of fate and helped put events in motion. She remained an important part of the story right from the start until the very end of the trilogy. From goading the main character into the self-realisation of his true nature and purpose in life to inspiring him to have faith while on the verge of death, she made things happen in whatever way she saw fit.

Like The Oracle, then, astrologers and astrology combined, is one of the many, many agents of our destinies. But whether we choose to pay attention to them or ignore them, they are likely not going away anytime soon because their raison d'etre—the nature of human destiny—is unlikely to ever change. And that is important for us because as the Czech writer Milan Kundera put it, chance and chance alone has a message for us because it is the only thing in our experience of life that speaks to us.

Notes

1   Fritjof Capra, *The Tao of Physics* (Harper Collins Flamingo, 1982), p. 39.
2   Ibid., p. 339.